As we plant flowers or a garden, we spend each day providing that new seedling with what it needs to produce the best fruit, flower or plant that it can. We understand that when we use the best soil, ensure adequate sunlight and constant watering, we are allowing that seed to grow into something beautiful.

The same thing happens when we plant our faith in the best soil, which is God's word. Ensure adequate sunlight, which is being surrounded by other believers. The constant watering, which is the time we spend daily with Christ. This allows our lives to grow into something beautiful.

Daily Nourishing provides us an opportunity to ensure we spend that precious time with God on a daily basis. You will read scripture, answer questions, complete activities and write down your thoughts daily (sort of like taking notes in Sunday school). As the year progresses you can track your progress and see how much you've grown. Each day provides a different activity and a different opportunity to move closer to Christ.

We hope you thoroughly enjoy being nourished and sharing that nourishment with those around you. Our goal is to plant a garden of believers that produces more and more fruit each year.

God Bless you and may every day of your life be filled with Nourishment.

- The Bethea Family

Day 1

1 John 4 (New King James Version)

⁷ Beloved, let us love one another, for love is of God; and everyone who loves is born of God and knows God. ⁸ He who does not love does not know God, for God is love. ⁹ In this the love of God was manifested toward us, that God has sent His only begotten Son into the world, that we might live through Him. ¹⁰ In this is love, not that we loved God, but that He loved us and sent His Son to be the propitiation for our sins. ¹¹ Beloved, if God so loved us, we also ought to love one another.

1. What steps will you take to be a more loving person today?
2. Is there something preventing you from loving a friend? A co-worker? Your Spouse?
3. Knowing that God is love and understanding that Jesus was sacrificed because of that love, are you moving closer to love or closer to the world?
4. Is your inability to love or just get along with someone due to your inability to forgive them?

Ways I can change are…..

_____
_____
_____
_____
_____

My feelings about this Scripture are……

_____
_____
_____
_____
_____

Starting Tomorrow I'm going to……

_____
_____
_____
_____
_____

Day 2

Deuteronomy 1 (New King James Version)

²⁹ "Then I said to you, 'Do not be terrified, or afraid of them. ³⁰ The LORD your God, who goes before you, He will fight for you, according to all He did for you in Egypt before your eyes, ³¹ and in the wilderness where you saw how the LORD your God carried you, as a man carries his son, in all the way that you went until you came to this place.' ³² Yet, for all that, you did not believe the LORD your God, ³³ who went in the way before you to search out a place for you to pitch your tents, to show you the way you should go, in the fire by night and in the cloud by day.

1. How many times has God fought for you, yet you still fear everything?
2. Although God has gone ahead of you and provided a place to pitch your tent, do you still attempt to pitch your tent in other places?
3. "In the fire by night and in the cloud by day", suggest that God is always guiding us. How often do you wait for God to show you the right path? How often do you follow the path that is the short cut to what you want?
4. In the "wilderness" or in bad times we see how God has taken care of us, so why is it so difficult to follow him when things are going great?

My thoughts on this Scripture……

_____
_____
_____
_____
_____   _____

My biggest fear in trusting God is…..

_____
_____
_____
_____

Lord I love you, please help me with…..

_____
_____
_____
_____
_____

Day 3

Matthew 27 (New King James Version)

24 When Pilate saw that he could not prevail at all, but rather that a tumult was rising, he took water and washed his hands before the multitude, saying, "I am innocent of the blood of this just Person.[d] You see to it."

25 And all the people answered and said, "His blood be on us and on our children."

26 Then he released Barabbas to them; and when he had scourged Jesus, he delivered Him to be crucified.

If you know this story you know that Pilate, the governor, provided the crowd an opportunity to choose Jesus but they chose someone else. Not much has changed today. We are given an opportunity to choose Jesus but we choose money, power or fame. And much like then, the majority of the people didn't make a decision based on what they knew, they were persuaded by others. Many people today would rather be led by someone else's beliefs rather than spend time trying to find something they believe in.

And yes, that *is* what I'm doing as well. I am trying to get you to believe that God is your Savior but I'm also trying to get you to read, research and understand for yourself. Verse 25 *"And all the people answered and said, "His blood be on us and on our children."* To not know what you are condemning your life for and to add that to the life of your children is unbelievable. Please take some time out of your day and find out about God. If afterwards you still don't want to believe, at least it was your decision.

What I think of this Scripture….

_____
_____
_____
_____

My beliefs _are_ my own because I…..

_____
_____
_____
_____
_____

Day 4

1 Corinthians 2 (New King James Version)

⁹ But as it is written:

"Eye has not seen, nor ear heard,
Nor have entered into the heart of man
The things which God has prepared for those who love Him."[c]

1. If you found out you had a wealthy relative that passed and you were in the will, how much would you be willing to go through to find out what they left you?
2. You don't doubt God has gifts for you in heaven but you want to get all you can get while you're here too, right? Why?
3. If God has provided for you and you have not been obedient, how could you not want to know what he has for you once you truly love him?
4. This scripture means you've never thought about the things God has for you and all you have to do is prepare your life to receive them.

What I think about this Scripture…

_____
_____
_____
_____
_____

I will prepare my life to receive Him by….

_____
_____
_____
_____

Knowing God has great plans for my life makes me…

_____
_____
_____
_____

Day 5

Deuteronomy 1 (New King James Version)

⁴² "And the LORD said to me, 'Tell them, "Do not go up nor fight, for I am not among you; lest you be defeated before your enemies." ⁴³ So I spoke to you; yet you would not listen, but rebelled against the command of the LORD, and presumptuously went up into the mountain. ⁴⁴ And the Amorites who dwelt in that mountain came out against you and chased you as bees do, and drove you back from Seir to Hormah. ⁴⁵ Then you returned and wept before the LORD, but the LORD would not listen to your voice nor give ear to you.

Take a moment to write about a time in your life when you knew you were going against the will of God.

_____

_____

_____

_____

_____

_____

1. Even if it worked out okay for you did you feel any guilt knowing you were not obeying God's will?
2. Did you ask God for forgiveness afterwards or were you too ashamed?
3. Will you listen more closely to hear what God is saying to you? Why or why not?

_____

_____

_____

4. Do you feel people sometimes assume God will help them even when they know they aren't being obedient?

To avoid being "chased as bees do" in the future I plan to...

_____

_____

_____

_____

Day 6

Exodus 15 (New King James Version)

22 So Moses brought Israel from the Red Sea; then they went out into the Wilderness of Shur. And they went three days in the wilderness and found no water. 23 Now when they came to Marah, they could not drink the waters of Marah, for they were bitter. Therefore the name of it was called Marah.[a] 24 And the people complained against Moses, saying, "What shall we drink?" 25 So he cried out to the LORD, and the LORD showed him a tree. When he cast it into the waters, the waters were made sweet.

There He made a statute and an ordinance for them, and there He tested them, 26 and said, "If you diligently heed the voice of the LORD your God and do what is right in His sight, give ear to His commandments and keep all His statutes, I will put none of the diseases on you which I have brought on the Egyptians. For I am the LORD who heals you."

1. Do you focus on how God is changing your life or are you too busy complaining about other things?
2. In the mist of it all, Moses cried out to the Lord. Do you?
3. Will you heed his voice? Will you do what is right? Will you hear His commandments? Will you keep His statutes?

What I think about this Scripture….

_____

_____

_____

_____

Write about what God *is* doing in your life and what you *want* God to do in your life

_____

_____

_____

_____

_____

_____

_____

_____

_____

Day 7

Jonah 1 (New King James Version)

¹⁵ So they picked up Jonah and threw him into the sea, and the sea ceased from its raging. ¹⁶ Then the men feared the LORD exceedingly, and offered a sacrifice to the LORD and took vows.

A verse or two before this, these men were praying to other gods. But the sea became more violent. Jonah explained that by throwing him into the sea, his Lord would spare their lives and calm the sea. By hearing this, by doing this and by seeing this, these men became believers of the _only_ living God.
 Something truly amazing that I think people overlook, this is not an ideal time for Jonah but he was still converting souls.

1. Would you have helped throw Jonah into the sea knowing it would save your life?
2. To have someone tell you about the power of the Lord and then witness it for yourself, would that have convinced you to give your life to Christ?
3. Really? Okay, well this is me telling you about the power of the Lord and I know you've already witnessed it, so……

I'll let you go so you can talk to God……………. **Congratulations!**

My thoughts about this Scripture…..

_____
_____
_____
_____
_____

What caused me to take my vows……

_____
_____
_____
_____
_____

Day 8

Ecclesiastes 12 (New King James Version)

Fear God and keep His commandments,
For this is man's all.
[14] For God will bring every work into judgment,
Including every secret thing,
Whether good or evil.

Do you feel sometimes you've outsmarted God? That maybe you've gotten away with something that you'll never have to deal with again? Well I hate to be the bearer of bad news but you haven't. God doesn't expect us to never do anything wrong, however He does expect us to do the right thing afterwards. When you, with a sincere heart, ask God to forgive you he does. Now, Satan will make you believe that somehow God missed that thing you did last night or that if you don't bring it up maybe God will forget about it.

Let's face it, God is pretty busy. So maybe he did miss that you are not being......Okay, I'll stop writing it if you stop believing it.

1. I ask God to forgive me of my sins everyday, even if I don't remember committing any. [ ] True   [ ] False
2. I am weak at times but I don't try to keep anything from God, I just ask for strength to help me deal with it. [ ] True   [ ] False
3. The "Fear of God" is a fear of being disobedient and not following God's word. It is not a fear that keeps you from calling on Him in times of need.
[ ] True   [ ] False

If I will be judged on everything, good or evil, I need to....

_____
_____
_____
_____
_____

A secrete should be kept because of its confidentiality, not because of shame.

I agree because

_____
_____

I disagree because

_____
_____
_____

Day 9

Romans 8 (New King James Version)

37 Yet in all these things we are more than conquerors through Him who loved us.
38 For I am persuaded that neither death nor life, nor angels nor principalities nor powers, nor things present nor things to come, 39 nor height nor depth, nor any other created thing, shall be able to separate us from the love of God which is in Christ Jesus our Lord.

Please understand that this Scripture is telling us that regardless of what we have or what we may have later, we must still love God more. No matter how much we *gain* in our lives, we must care more about our relationship with Him. No matter how many thing we *loose* during our lives, we must care more about our relationship with Him. And with that love for the Lord, we will be conquerors.

Create a list of things in your life making number 1 the most important thing and 20 the least important thing. Remember, be honest.

1.
2.
3.
4.
5.
6.
7.
8.
9.
10.
11.
12.
13.
14.
15.
16.
17.
18.
19.
20.

Day 10

Revelation 3 (New King James Version)

Because you have kept My command to persevere, I also will keep you from the hour of trial which shall come upon the whole world, to test those who dwell on the earth.
[11] Behold,[e] I am coming quickly! Hold fast what you have, that no one may take your crown. [12] He who overcomes, I will make him a pillar in the temple of My God, and he shall go out no more. I will write on him the name of My God and the name of the city of My God, the New Jerusalem, which comes down out of heaven from My God. And I will write on him My new name.

As I read this Scripture I think about…

_____
_____
_____
_____
_____

Starting today I will_____ because I want God to keep me from the hour of trial. I _____ the Lord and I will _____ His commandments. We may not know the _____ or _____ that He will return, but we do know by this scripture He is coming _____. Now since we have no concept of God's time, He could return _____ or _____ maybe even_____, we just need to be ready. The Bible is my_____ and when I read it I better understand _____. I also love how different verses _____ to my life today. I try not to _____ to my friends but I do _____ God and often mention _____ because without Him I could not have made it through _____.

1. Do you check yourself daily in order to make sure you are keeping God's commandments?
2. Do you own anything that keeps you from truly loving God?
3. If you died today still loving the things of this world, nothing you have would go with you. However, if you give up everything you have for God, everything you need would be waiting for you. So will you answer number 2 again?

. We spend so much time on earth trying to belong to exclusive clubs and live in the best neighborhoods. To have the name of God and the city of God written on us represents who we belong to and where we will live, well as the saying goes "It don't get no better than this".

Day 11

Psalm 108 (New King James Version)

O God, my heart is steadfast;
I will sing and give praise, even with my glory.
² Awake, lute and harp!
I will awaken the dawn.
³ I will praise You, O LORD, among the peoples,
And I will sing praises to You among the nations.
⁴ For Your mercy is great above the heavens,
And Your truth reaches to the clouds.

1. When we get to heaven it will be to praise God and glorify His name, right? So, why not start here? If you are ashamed to praise Him now, what in the world are you going to do when you get to heaven?
2. Having a steadfast heart means you don't wavier back and forth about how you feel about our Lord. What happens during your day to make you unsure about how you feel about God?
3. Are you willing to sing praises from the time you rise until you fall asleep?

Try this today. Regardless of what anyone says to you, you will not get upset. I know sounds impossible but just try it. Your goal is to get control over your emotions so Satan can't tempt your steadfast heart. Your motivation is that joy deep down inside you that comes from knowing how much God loves.

I praise God by….

_____
_____
_____
_____

This scripture motivates me to…..

_____
_____
_____
_____
_____
_____
_____

Day 12

Job 27 (New King James Version)

[11] "I will teach you about the hand of God;
What is with the Almighty I will not conceal.
[12] Surely all of you have seen it;
Why then do you behave with complete nonsense?

As adults we know right from wrong. We know what we should be doing and how to treat people. However, we tend to do right when it is convenient for us. We treat people well when it benefits us. This behavior is not limited to the nonbeliever but those of us who claim to know the Lord, those of us calling ourselves Christians or wanting to be true representatives of God are behaving with complete nonsense. The goodness of the Almighty has not been concealed from us, so if He is in us, *that* should not be concealed.

1. What can you do to teach people about the hand of God?
2. Is what you say completely different from how you act when it comes to your Christian walk?
3. If God's goodness has been revealed to you, why do you continue to mistreat people?
4. Do you believe that the "nonsense" mentioned above also pertains to things we do to ourselves? (doubt, fear, laziness)

My feelings about the scripture…

_____
_____
_____
_____
_____

I say I'm a Christian and my actions…..

_____
_____
_____

Being doubtful, fearful or lazy is nonsense because….

_____
_____
_____
_____
_____

Day 13

Proverbs 1 (New King James Version)

1 The proverbs of Solomon the son of David, king of Israel:

2 To know wisdom and instruction,
To perceive the words of understanding,
3 To receive the instruction of wisdom,
Justice, judgment, and equity;
4 To give prudence to the simple,
To the young man knowledge and discretion—
5 A wise man will hear and increase learning,
And a man of understanding will attain wise counsel,
6 To understand a proverb and an enigma,
The words of the wise and their riddles.
7 The fear of the LORD is the beginning of knowledge,
But fools despise wisdom and instruction.

1. Are you so full of the Lord that you don't think there is anything anyone can teach you?
2. If Solomon with all his wisdom, knowledge and wealth still understood he was nothing without the Lord, why is it so hard for us to see?
3. Do you think this scripture suggest that we should not only attain wise counsel but provide it as well?

If yes, how do we become wiser?

_____
_____
_____

If no, what do you do with the wisdom you have?

_____
_____
_____

After reading this scripture I think...

_____
_____
_____
_____

Day 14

Joel 3 (New King James Version)

¹⁴ Multitudes, multitudes in the valley of decision!
For the day of the LORD is near in the valley of decision.
¹⁵ The sun and moon will grow dark,
And the stars will diminish their brightness.
¹⁶ The LORD also will roar from Zion,
And utter His voice from Jerusalem;
The heavens and earth will shake;
But the LORD will be a shelter for His people,
And the strength of the children of Israel.

¹⁷ "So you shall know that I am the LORD your God,
Dwelling in Zion My holy mountain.
Then Jerusalem shall be holy,
And no aliens shall ever pass through her again."

We often hear that Jesus is coming to save those who love him and who have kept his commandments. I wonder if because it has been mentioned so many times in the Bible and He has not returned yet, that people continue to delay giving their lives to Christ. They feel they have time or that there are so many things they have to do first.

Use today as your day of decision. You decide today that you are going to allow the Lord to be your shelter. You decide that you want to be INSIDE the walls of Jerusalem and not be an alien who cannot pass through.

My Decision…

_____
_____
_____
_____
_____
_____
_____
_____
_____
_____
_____

Day 15

John 3 (New King James Version)

16 For God so loved the world that He gave His only begotten Son, that whoever believes in Him should not perish but have everlasting life. 17 For God did not send His Son into the world to condemn the world, but that the world through Him might be saved.

Lord! Thank you!

To show I love you Lord today I will…

1. _____
2. _____
3. _____
4. _____
5. _____
6. _____
7. _____
8. _____
9. _____
10. _____

To show I love you Lord today I did….

1. _____
2. _____
3. _____
4. _____
5. _____
6. _____
7. _____
8. _____
9. _____
10. _____

Lord,

Thank you for this day that *You* provided, so I could show *You* how much I love You!

Day 16

Acts 4 (New King James Version)

31 And when they had prayed, the place where they were assembled together was shaken; and they were all filled with the Holy Spirit, and they spoke the word of God with boldness.

The power of prayer is amazing. To speak to God, to ask of your God and believe in your heart that it will be done, is a wonderful thing.

1. What will you ask of God today?
2. The Bible tells us that where ever two are more gather in Jesus' name, He will be in the mist. Who will you pray with today?
3. Who will you pray for today
4. Do you know God's word well enough to speak it boldly to someone else?
5. If you don't know God's word, will you learn at least one scripture and learn it well?

When I read this scripture I....

_____
_____
_____
_____
_____

Can you remember one time when you were filled with the Holy Spirit?

_____
_____
_____
_____
_____
_____
_____

Day 17

James 2 (New King James Version)

2 My brethren, do not hold the faith of our Lord Jesus Christ, the Lord of glory, with partiality. ² For if there should come into your assembly a man with gold rings, in fine apparel, and there should also come in a poor man in filthy clothes, ³ and you pay attention to the one wearing the fine clothes and say to him, "You sit here in a good place," and say to the poor man, "You stand there," or, "Sit here at my footstool," ⁴ have you not shown partiality among yourselves, and become judges with evil thoughts?

⁵ Listen, my beloved brethren: Has God not chosen the poor of this world to be rich in faith and heirs of the kingdom which He promised to those who love Him? ⁶ But you have dishonored the poor man. Do not the rich oppress you and drag you into the courts? ⁷ Do they not blaspheme that noble name by which you are called?

⁸ If you really fulfill the royal law according to the Scripture, "You shall love your neighbor as yourself,"[a] you do well; ⁹ but if you show partiality, you commit sin, and are convicted by the law as transgressors. ¹⁰ For whoever shall keep the whole law, and yet stumble in one point, he is guilty of all. ¹¹ For He who said, "Do not commit adultery,"[b] also said, "Do not murder."[c] Now if you do not commit adultery, but you do murder, you have become a transgressor of the law. ¹² So speak and so do as those who will be judged by the law of liberty. ¹³ For judgment is without mercy to the one who has shown no mercy. Mercy triumphs over judgment.

1. Do you feel it is possible to advance in your job and not show partiality or favoritism to someone?
2. Have you used the wrong someone else is doing, to diminish the wrong you're doing?
3. Do you base your success on the success of your family and friends?
4. Do you compare your accomplishments with others to determine if they meet the standards of being your friend?
5. Will you or did you pick your spouse based on job title or income? (no it isn't a sin but it shows you do put people in classes)

This scripture....

_____
_____
_____
_____

Day 18

Mark 10 (New King James Version)

17 Now as He was going out on the road, one came running, knelt before Him, and asked Him, "Good Teacher, what shall I do that I may inherit eternal life?"

18 So Jesus said to him, "Why do you call Me good? No one is good but One, that is, God. 19 You know the commandments: 'Do not commit adultery,' 'Do not murder,' 'Do not steal,' 'Do not bear false witness,' 'Do not defraud,' 'Honor your father and your mother.'"[c]

20 And he answered and said to Him, "Teacher, all these things I have kept from my youth."

21 Then Jesus, looking at him, loved him, and said to him, "One thing you lack: Go your way, sell whatever you have and give to the poor, and you will have treasure in heaven; and come, take up the cross, and follow Me."

22 But he was sad at this word, and went away sorrowful, for he had great possessions.

1. Are you willing to give up everything for eternal life?
2. Do you consider yourself "good" because you keep a few commandments?
3. When you ask Jesus a question are you prepared for the answer?

I want to change my…

_____
_____
_____
_____

My possessions mean….

_____
_____

my chance at eternal life is….

_____
_____
_____
_____

Day 19

Luke 2 (New King James Version)

[13] And suddenly there was with the angel a multitude of the heavenly host praising God and saying:

*[14] "Glory to God in the highest,
And on earth peace, goodwill toward men!"[c]*

*You create peace in your life today.

*You control your emotions and they will not be controlled by the things around you today

*You know that God is in control of your life, stop worrying today.

*There will be no stress for you today.

*You will mend a broken friendship today

*You will give everything to God today.

Today will be a "Glory to God" type day!

I will make today a great day by...

_____
_____
_____
_____
_____

To get peace you must give peace so I will stop...

_____
_____
_____
_____
_____

Day 20

Ecclesiastes 2 (New King James Version)

2 I said in my heart, "Come now, I will test you with mirth; therefore enjoy pleasure"; but surely, this also was vanity. [2] I said of laughter—"Madness!"; and of mirth, "What does it accomplish?" [3] I searched in my heart how to gratify my flesh with wine, while guiding my heart with wisdom, and how to lay hold on folly, till I might see what was good for the sons of men to do under heaven all the days of their lives.

[4] I made my works great, I built myself houses, and planted myself vineyards. [5] I made myself gardens and orchards, and I planted all kinds of fruit trees in them. [6] I made myself water pools from which to water the growing trees of the grove. [7] I acquired male and female servants, and had servants born in my house. Yes, I had greater possessions of herds and flocks than all who were in Jerusalem before me. [8] I also gathered for myself silver and gold and the special treasures of kings and of the provinces. I acquired male and female singers, the delights of the sons of men, and musical instruments[a] of all kinds.

[26] For God gives wisdom and knowledge and joy to a man who is good in His sight; but to the sinner He gives the work of gathering and collecting, that he may give to him who is good before God. This also is vanity and grasping for the wind.

We will never be as wealthy as Solomon. We will not have his power, his wisdom nor accomplish the things he did. Yet, Solomon's claim in this scripture is that as hard as he tried he could not fill his void with material things. To love the Lord, to glorify His name to make Him first in his life was more fulfilling than anything he could buy.
So, I ask you, if Solomon could not buy his way out of his need for God, what chance do we have?

This scripture…..

_____
_____
_____
_____
_____

When I fill empty or without something I ….

_____
_____
_____
_____
_____

Day 21

Romans 5 (New King James Version)

⁸ But God demonstrates His own love toward us, in that while we were still sinners, Christ died for us. ⁹ Much more then, having now been justified by His blood, we shall be saved from wrath through Him. ¹⁰ For if when we were enemies we were reconciled to God through the death of His Son, much more, having been reconciled, we shall be saved by His life. ¹¹ And not only that, but we also rejoice in God through our Lord Jesus Christ, through whom we have now received the reconciliation.

After reading this scripture I feel I should...

_____
_____
_____
_____
_____

To know that Christ died for me even when I was still a sinner is...

_____
_____
_____
_____
_____

If you ever doubted God's love for you, does this scripture help?

How?

_____
_____
_____
_____

No, because...

_____
_____
_____
_____
_____

Day 22

Proverbs 17 (New King James Version)

⁴ An evildoer gives heed to false lips;
A liar listens eagerly to a spiteful tongue

⁵ He who mocks the poor reproaches his Maker;
He who is glad at calamity will not go unpunished.

What is your understanding of verse 4?

_____
_____
_____
_____

What is your understanding of verse 5?

_____
_____
_____
_____

How do you avoid both?

_____
_____
_____
_____
_____
_____
_____

Day 23

Titus 2 (New King James Version)

11 For the grace of God that brings salvation has appeared to all men, 12 teaching us that, denying ungodliness and worldly lusts, we should live soberly, righteously, and godly in the present age, 13 looking for the blessed hope and glorious appearing of our great God and Savior Jesus Christ, 14 who gave Himself for us, that He might redeem us from every lawless deed and purify for Himself His own special people, zealous for good works.

15 Speak these things, exhort, and rebuke with all authority. Let no one despise you.

We have a good understanding of how we should live. We are well equipped with the knowledge of right and wrong. When you look to see if anyone is watching before you take money from the register at work, when you meet another woman's husband in a dark parking lot or when you cut off the lights and close your door so you can log on to that special website. The fact that you are sneaking means you know you are wrong. Although Jesus Christ was a sacrifice to redeem us from every lawless deed, we are still responsible to change our way of living. It is up to us to change our way of thinking. We are given the spiritual assistance to fight off the enemies advances. The biggest obstacle we face is not Satan but our will to change.

What steps will you take to change today?

_____
_____
_____
_____
_____
_____
_____

The phrase "Let no one despise you" to me means…

_____
_____
_____
_____
_____

Day 24

Jude 1 (New King James Version)

[12] These are spots in your love feasts, while they feast with you without fear, serving only themselves. They are clouds without water, carried about[c] by the winds; late autumn trees without fruit, twice dead, pulled up by the roots; [13] raging waves of the sea, foaming up their own shame; wandering stars for whom is reserved the blackness of darkness forever.

[14] Now Enoch, the seventh from Adam, prophesied about these men also, saying, "Behold, the Lord comes with ten thousands of His saints, [15] to execute judgment on all, to convict all who are ungodly among them of all their ungodly deeds which they have committed in an ungodly way, and of all the harsh things which ungodly sinners have spoken against Him."

[16] These are grumblers, complainers, walking according to their own lusts; and they mouth great swelling words, flattering people to gain advantage. [17] But you, beloved, remember the words which were spoken before by the apostles of our Lord Jesus Christ: [18] how they told you that there would be mockers in the last time who would walk according to their own ungodly lusts. [19] These are sensual persons, who cause divisions, not having the Spirit.

When I read this scripture I thing about….

_____
_____
_____
_____
_____
_____
_____
_____

Not only will I be cautious of these men, I will be careful not to become one of them.

Day 25

Genesis 19 (New King James Version)

* Then the men said to Lot, "Have you anyone else here? Son-in-law, your sons, your daughters, and whomever you have in the city—take them out of this place! ¹³ For we will destroy this place, because the outcry against them has grown great before the face of the LORD, and the LORD has sent us to destroy it."*

¹⁴ So Lot went out and spoke to his sons-in-law, who had married his daughters, and said, "Get up, get out of this place; for the LORD will destroy this city!" But to his sons-in-law he seemed to be joking.

¹⁵ When the morning dawned, the angels urged Lot to hurry, saying, "Arise, take your wife and your two daughters who are here, lest you be consumed in the punishment of the city." ¹⁶ And while he lingered, the men took hold of his hand, his wife's hand, and the hands of his two daughters, the LORD being merciful to him, and they brought him out and set him outside the city. ¹⁷ So it came to pass, when they had brought them outside, that he[a] said, "Escape for your life! Do not look behind you nor stay anywhere in the plain. Escape to the mountains, lest you be destroyed."

Even in a place that was corrupt, Lot remained obedient to God. Even in a place that was corrupt, God was still merciful to Lot. Where you live or who you live around should not determine your obedience nor does it limit God's mercy.

This scripture reminds me of….

_____
_____
_____
_____

Although I am aware of what is going on around me I …..

_____
_____
_____
_____

Day 28

James 4 (New King James Version)

13 Come now, you who say, "Today or tomorrow we will[g] go to such and such a city, spend a year there, buy and sell, and make a profit"; 14 whereas you do not know what will happen tomorrow. For what is your life? It is even a vapor that appears for a little time and then vanishes away. 15 Instead you ought to say, "If the Lord wills, we shall live and do this or that." 16 But now you boast in your arrogance. All such boasting is evil.

17 Therefore, to him who knows to do good and does not do it, to him it is sin.

1. How long have you put off being saved?
2. If you hurt someone today, should you put off apologizing until tomorrow?
3. If you knew there was no tomorrow, would you give your life to Christ today?
4. When you ask God for things, do you ever say "Lord if it is your will?"
5. If you have your future planned out. You know what you want to do, you know where you want to go and those plans do not include God. How well do you think you've planned them?

This scripture is…..

_____
_____
_____
_____
_____

When I make plans I…..

_____
_____
_____
_____

Day 27

Luke 24 (New King James Version)

Now on the first day of the week, very early in the morning, they, and certain other women with them,[a] came to the tomb bringing the spices which they had prepared. 2 But they found the stone rolled away from the tomb. 3 Then they went in and did not find the body of the Lord Jesus. 4 And it happened, as they were greatly[b] perplexed about this, that behold, two men stood by them in shining garments. 5 Then, as they were afraid and bowed their faces to the earth, they said to them, "Why do you seek the living among the dead? 6 He is not here, but is risen! Remember how He spoke to you when He was still in Galilee, 7 saying, 'The Son of Man must be delivered into the hands of sinful men, and be crucified, and the third day rise again.'"

8 And they remembered His words. 9 Then they returned from the tomb and told all these things to the eleven and to all the rest. 10 It was Mary Magdalene, Joanna, Mary the mother of James, and the other women with them, who told these things to the apostles. 11 And their words seemed to them like idle tales, and they did not believe them. 12 But Peter arose and ran to the tomb; and stooping down, he saw the linen cloths lying[c] by themselves; and he departed, marveling to himself at what had happened.

Now, when we say we are saved, Christians, believers or followers of Christ, what we mean is we are believers of this scripture. We believe Jesus died on the cross for our sins and rose again on the third day.

I believe that...

_____

_____

_____

_____

_____

When I read this I…

_____

_____

_____

_____

_____

Day 28

Revelation 22 (New King James Version)

⁶ Then he said to me, "These words are faithful and true." And the Lord God of the holy[b] prophets sent His angel to show His servants the things which must shortly take place.

⁷ "Behold, I am coming quickly! Blessed is he who keeps the words of the prophecy of this book."

⁸ Now I, John, saw and heard[c] these things. And when I heard and saw, I fell down to worship before the feet of the angel who showed me these things.

⁹ Then he said to me, "See that you do not do that. For[d] I am your fellow servant, and of your brethren the prophets, and of those who keep the words of this book. Worship God." ¹⁰ And he said to me, "Do not seal the words of the prophecy of this book, for the time is at hand. ¹¹ He who is unjust, let him be unjust still; he who is filthy, let him be filthy still; he who is righteous, let him be righteous[e] still; he who is holy, let him be holy still."

1. Are you cautious of people who wished to be idolized or worshiped?
2. Do you spend so much time trying to save others that you've forgotten to save yourself?
3. Is the Bible your source of guidance through all things or just a few?
4. Very few of us will experience what John did but do you ever feel you're being given direction?

This scripture gives me….

_____

_____

_____

_____

_____

Day 29

Numbers 13 (New King James Version)

³⁰ Then Caleb quieted the people before Moses, and said, "Let us go up at once and take possession, for we are well able to overcome it."

³¹ But the men who had gone up with him said, "We are not able to go up against the people, for they are stronger than we." ³² And they gave the children of Israel a bad report of the land which they had spied out, saying, "The land through which we have gone as spies is a land that devours its inhabitants, and all the people whom we saw in it are men of great stature. ³³ There we saw the giants[d] (the descendants of Anak came from the giants); and we were like grasshoppers in our own sight, and so we were in their sight."

Have you ever wanted something really bad? You prayed about it and from your understanding God said yes and provide you a way to get it. However, people around you talked so bad about it, gave you all these reasons why you shouldn't have it. And, you listened to the people and not God. There is an old saying, "If God will bring you to it He will bring you through it". (That saying may be limited to us country folk) But it is true. God has things planned for our lives and all of them are good. Now, we may have to go through a few bad things to get to the good but that should only make you appreciate it more.

!. Can you think of a time you let someone talk you out of something that you were sure was meant for you?
2. Are you more focused now on God's voice and not the voice of people?
3. Will you allow yourself to believe that there is some land that God has just for you and your obedience will ensure you receive it?

I plan to..

_____
_____
_____
_____
_____

Day 30

It has been thirty days,

I feel I have…

_____
_____
_____
_____
_____
_____
_____

I still want to..

_____
_____
_____
_____
_____
_____

My faith and understanding has..

_____
_____
_____
_____
_____
_____

Day 31

Matthew 6; Matthew 9 (New King James Version)

"And when you pray, you shall not be like the hypocrites. For they love to pray standing in the synagogues and on the corners of the streets, that they may be seen by men. Assuredly, I say to you, they have their reward. [6] But you, when you pray, go into your room, and when you have shut your door, pray to your Father who is in the secret place; and your Father who sees in secret will reward you openly.[b] [7] And when you pray, do not use vain repetitions as the heathen do. For they think that they will be heard for their many words.

[8] "Therefore do not be like them. For your Father knows the things you have need of before you ask Him. [9] In this manner, therefore, pray:

Our Father in heaven,
Hallowed be Your name.
[10] Your kingdom come.
Your will be done
On earth as it is in heaven.
[11] Give us this day our daily bread.
[12] And forgive us our debts,
As we forgive our debtors.
[13] And do not lead us into temptation,
But deliver us from the evil one.
For Yours is the kingdom and the power and the glory forever. Amen.[c]

[14] "For if you forgive men their trespasses, your heavenly Father will also forgive you. [15] But if you do not forgive men their trespasses, neither will your Father forgive your trespasses.

1. When you pray do you pray to God or do you pray for man?
2. Do you consider what you are praying for to ensure you are not just filling daily cravings that will leave you unfulfilled tomorrow?
3. Are you being sincere when you pray?
4. Do your prayers only consist of things for you?
5. Do you include "If it's your will" in your prayers?

Write your prayer here…

_____
_____
_____
_____
_____
_____

Day 32

Deuteronomy 5 (New King James Version)

⁶ 'I am the L ORD your God who brought you out of the land of Egypt, out of the house of bondage.

⁷ 'You shall have no other gods before Me.

⁸ 'You shall not make for yourself a carved image—any likeness of anything that is in heaven above, or that is in the earth beneath, or that is in the water under the earth; ⁹ you shall not bow down to them nor serve them. For I, the L ORD your God, am a jealous God, visiting the iniquity of the fathers upon the children to the third and fourth generations of those who hate Me, ¹⁰ but showing mercy to thousands, to those who love Me and keep My commandments.

¹¹ 'You shall not take the name of the L ORD your God in vain, for the L ORD will not hold him guiltless who takes His name in vain.

¹⁶ 'Honor your father and your mother, as the L ORD your God has commanded you, that your days may be long, and that it may be well with you in the land which the L ORD your God is giving you.

¹⁷ 'You shall not murder.

¹⁸ 'You shall not commit adultery.

¹⁹ 'You shall not steal.

²⁰ 'You shall not bear false witness against your neighbor.

²¹ 'You shall not covet your neighbor's wife; and you shall not desire your neighbor's house, his field, his male servant, his female servant, his ox, his donkey, or anything that is your neighbor's.'

Instead of always telling God what we want or what we require, sometimes it does us good to hear what He requires.

Day 33

Deuteronomy 28 (New King James Version)

"Now it shall come to pass, if you diligently obey the voice of the LORD your God, to observe carefully all His commandments which I command you today, that the LORD your God will set you high above all nations of the earth. ² And all these blessings shall come upon you and overtake you, because you obey the voice of the LORD your God:

³ "Blessed shall you be in the city, and blessed shall you be in the country.

⁴ "Blessed shall be the fruit of your body, the produce of your ground and the increase of your herds, the increase of your cattle and the offspring of your flocks.

⁵ "Blessed shall be your basket and your kneading bowl.

⁶ "Blessed shall you be when you come in, and blessed shall you be when you go out.

⁷ "The LORD will cause your enemies who rise against you to be defeated before your face; they shall come out against you one way and flee before you seven ways.

⁸ "The LORD will command the blessing on you in your storehouses and in all to which you set your hand, and He will bless you in the land which the LORD your God is giving you.

⁹ "The LORD will establish you as a holy people to Himself, just as He has sworn to you, if you keep the commandments of the LORD your God and walk in His ways. ¹⁰ Then all peoples of the earth shall see that you are called by the name of the LORD, and they shall be afraid of you. ¹¹ And the LORD will grant you plenty of goods, in the fruit of your body, in the increase of your livestock, and in the produce of your ground, in the land of which the LORD swore to your fathers to give you. ¹² The LORD will open to you His good treasure, the heavens, to give the rain to your land in its season, and to bless all the work of your hand. You shall lend to many nations, but you shall not borrow. ¹³ And the LORD will make you the head and not the tail; you shall be above only, and not be beneath, if you heed the commandments of the LORD your God, which I command you today, and are careful to observe them. ¹⁴ So you shall not turn aside from any of the words which I command you this day, to the right or the left, to go after other gods to serve them.

God has so many things for us. He has so many blessings that He wants to give us. All He asked is that we be obedient and follow his word.

Day 34

Genesis 37 (New King James Version)

⁵ Now Joseph had a dream, and he told it to his brothers; and they hated him even more. ⁶ So he said to them, "Please hear this dream which I have dreamed: ⁷ There we were, binding sheaves in the field. Then behold, my sheaf arose and also stood upright; and indeed your sheaves stood all around and bowed down to my sheaf."

⁸ And his brothers said to him, "Shall you indeed reign over us? Or shall you indeed have dominion over us?" So they hated him even more for his dreams and for his words.

⁹ Then he dreamed still another dream and told it to his brothers, and said, "Look, I have dreamed another dream. And this time, the sun, the moon, and the eleven stars bowed down to me."

¹⁰ So he told it to his father and his brothers; and his father rebuked him and said to him, "What is this dream that you have dreamed? Shall your mother and I and your brothers indeed come to bow down to the earth before you?" ¹¹ And his brothers envied him, but his father kept the matter in mind

Those of you who know this story know that his father, mother and his brothers did bow down to him. His dreams came true regardless of who doubted him, it did not matter that he was hated. Even being mistreated could not stop what God had for him. Let this encourage you to keep your dreams even when you are the only one who believes in them.

1. What dreams do you have in your heart that you continue to put off because of fear?
2. Do you search for approval from your friends before you make major decisions in your own life?
3. God knows your heart. If you have a dream in your heart will you talk to God about it? With the two of you working on it together, how can it fail?

After reading this I..

_____
_____
_____
_____
_____

Day 35

Acts 9 (New King James Version)

Then Saul, still breathing threats and murder against the disciples of the Lord, went to the high priest [2] and asked letters from him to the synagogues of Damascus, so that if he found any who were of the Way, whether men or women, he might bring them bound to Jerusalem.

[3] As he journeyed he came near Damascus, and suddenly a light shone around him from heaven. [4] Then he fell to the ground, and heard a voice saying to him, "Saul, Saul, why are you persecuting Me?"

[5] And he said, "Who are You, Lord?"

Then the Lord said, "I am Jesus, whom you are persecuting.[a] It is hard for you to kick against the goads."

[6] So he, trembling and astonished, said, "Lord, what do You want me to do?"

Then the Lord said to him, "Arise and go into the city, and you will be told what you must do."

[7] And the men who journeyed with him stood speechless, hearing a voice but seeing no one. [8] Then Saul arose from the ground, and when his eyes were opened he saw no one. But they led him by the hand and brought him into Damascus. [9] And he was three days without sight, and neither ate nor drank.

Daily, without fail, Satan will tell you that you are not worthy of Jesus' mercy. Satan will try to convince you that your past is too sinful, too shameful for you to be saved. This scripture should remove any doubt you have about the mercy of our Lord Jesus Christ.

Reading this I believe…

_____
_____
_____
_____
_____

The mercy of the Lord is..

_____
_____
_____
_____

Day 36

Haggai 1 (New King James Version)

3 Then the word of the LORD came by Haggai the prophet, saying, 4 "Is it time for you yourselves to dwell in your paneled houses, and this temple[a] to lie in ruins?" 5 Now therefore, thus says the LORD of hosts: "Consider your ways!

6 "You have sown much, and bring in little;
You eat, but do not have enough;
You drink, but you are not filled with drink;
You clothe yourselves, but no one is warm;
And he who earns wages,
Earns wages to put into a bag with holes."

7 Thus says the LORD of hosts: "Consider your ways! 8 Go up to the mountains and bring wood and build the temple, that I may take pleasure in it and be glorified," says the LORD. 9 "You looked for much, but indeed it came to little; and when you brought it home, I blew it away. Why?" says the LORD of hosts. "Because of My house that is in ruins, while every one of you runs to his own house. 10 Therefore the heavens above you withhold the dew, and the earth withholds its fruit. 11 For I called for a drought on the land and the mountains, on the grain and the new wine and the oil, on whatever the ground brings forth, on men and livestock, and on all the labor of your hands."

1. Should the church you attend be based on how much money you make?
2. Is it wrong for you to live in a mansion but God's house is falling apart?
3. Do we not have enough because we are selfish and are not concerned about what God wants?
4. Would your tithing the way God requires prevent His house from lacking as well as ours?
5. Do you expect more from God than you are willing to give Him?

I tithe…

_____
_____
_____

When I have a chance I _____ at church

If no one was there to see I would [ ] pick up, [ ] leave, [ ] throw paper on the floor at church.

Day 37

Romans 13 (New King James Version)

Let every soul be subject to the governing authorities. For there is no authority except from God, and the authorities that exist are appointed by God. [2] Therefore whoever resists the authority resists the ordinance of God, and those who resist will bring judgment on themselves. [3] For rulers are not a terror to good works, but to evil. Do you want to be unafraid of the authority? Do what is good, and you will have praise from the same. [4] For he is God's minister to you for good. But if you do evil, be afraid; for he does not bear the sword in vain; for he is God's minister, an avenger to execute wrath on him who practices evil. [5] Therefore you must be subject, not only because of wrath but also for conscience' sake. [6] For because of this you also pay taxes, for they are God's ministers attending continually to this very thing. [7] Render therefore to all their due: taxes to whom taxes are due, customs to whom customs, fear to whom fear, honor to whom honor.

1. What authorities do you defy?
2. Even if you are not praised by the authorities over you, do you continue to work hard?
3. How often do you find yourself rebelling against authority, refusing to work, arriving late, being upset when someone ask you to do what you are getting paid to do?

I sometimes rebel because…

_____
_____
_____
_____

I don't think I ever associated the authority over me with God but now….

_____
_____
_____
_____

I believe that no matter how bad the authority or how little I agree with it, that if I continue to do what I know to be right, God will take care of me.

Yes because

_____
_____

No because

_____
_____

Day 38

Matthew 28 (New King James Version)

⁹ And as they went to tell His disciples,[b] behold, Jesus met them, saying, "Rejoice!" So they came and held Him by the feet and worshiped Him. ¹⁰ Then Jesus said to them, "Do not be afraid. Go and tell My brethren to go to Galilee, and there they will see Me."

The Soldiers Are Bribed

¹¹ Now while they were going, behold, some of the guard came into the city and reported to the chief priests all the things that had happened. ¹² When they had assembled with the elders and consulted together, they gave a large sum of money to the soldiers, ¹³ saying, "Tell them, 'His disciples came at night and stole Him away while we slept.' ¹⁴ And if this comes to the governor's ears, we will appease him and make you secure." ¹⁵ So they took the money and did as they were instructed; and this saying is commonly reported among the Jews until this day.

Like these soldiers, chief priests and elders who tried to convince these people that Jesus is not alive, you will have people in your life trying to convince you of the same thing. And when they do how will you handle it?

_____
_____
_____
_____
_____
_____
_____

To know that Jesus rose again is amazing but to know why he rose is..

_____
_____
_____
_____

Day 39

ACROSS

1 This Roman governor condemned Jesus
4 The disciple Peter's other name
7 She was Jesus' mother
9 He climbed a tree to see Jesus (drop "s")
12 This disciple was known as "Doubting___"
14 This disciple walked on water with Jesus
15 This man was the first Christian stoned to death
16 This disciple betrayed Jesus

DOWN

2 Jesus brought this man back to life
3 He tempted Jesus (2 words)
5 She found Jesus' tomb empty (2 words)
6 This disciple was a tax collector
8 Jesus visited the house of these sisters (2 words)
10 He had a vision and wrote in down in the Book of Revelation
11 John the ___
13 Christ
15 This man became known as Paul after Jesus spoke to him on the road to Damascus

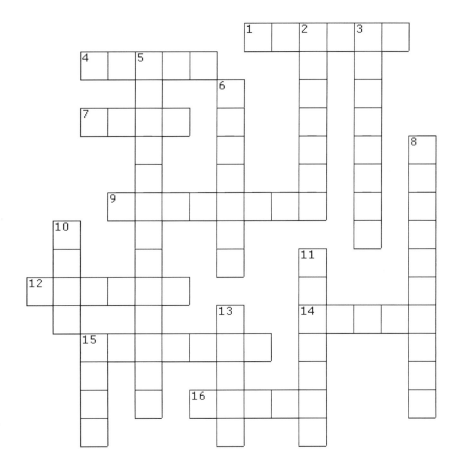

Day 40

1 Peter 1 (New King James Version)

25 But the word of the LORD endures forever."[g]

List the 66 Books of the Bible.

1.	34.
2.	35.
3.	36.
4.	37.
5.	38.
6.	39.
7.	40.
8.	41.
9.	42.
10.	43.
11.	44.
12.	45.
13.	46.
14.	47.
15.	48.
16.	49.
17.	50.
18.	51.
19.	52.
20.	53.
21.	54.
22.	55.
23.	56.
24.	57.
25.	58.
26.	59.
27.	60.
28.	61.
29.	62.
30.	63.
31.	64.
32.	65.
33.	66.

Day 41

Revelation 11 (New King James Version)

We give You thanks, O Lord God Almighty,
The One who is and who was and who is to come,[g]
Because You have taken Your great power and reigned.
18 The nations were angry, and Your wrath has come,
And the time of the dead, that they should be judged,
And that You should reward Your servants the prophets and the saints,
And those who fear Your name, small and great,
And should destroy those who destroy the earth."

When I read this I think about…

_____
_____
_____
_____
_____

When people do bad things shouldn't they expect to be held accountable?

_____
_____
_____
_____
_____

Do you think the scripture has a different meaning based on how you live your life?

Explain

_____
_____
_____
_____
_____

Day 42

Complete these scriptures

Exodus 7 (New King James Version)

*7 So the L*ORD *said to_____: "See, I have made you as God to_____, and _____your brother shall be your prophet. ² You shall speak all that I _____ you. And Aaron your _____ shall tell Pharaoh to send the children of_____ out of his land. ³ And I will _____ Pharaoh's heart, and multiply My _____ and My _____ in the land of Egypt. ⁴ But _____ will not heed you, so that I may lay My hand on _____ and bring My armies and My people, the _____ of Israel, out of the land of Egypt by great _____. ⁵ And the Egyptians shall know that I am the _____, when I _____ out My hand on Egypt and bring out the _____ ___ _____ from among them."*

Deuteronomy 6 (New King James Version)

*¹⁶ "You shall not tempt the _____ your _____ as you tempted Him in _____. ¹⁷ You shall _____ keep the _____ of the L*ORD *your God, His _____, and His _____ which He has commanded you. ¹⁸ And you shall do what is _____ and _____ in the sight of the _____, that it may be well with you, and that you may go in and _____ the good land of which the L*ORD *swore to your _____, ¹⁹ to cast out all your _____ from before you, as the L*ORD *has _____.*

Matthew 4 (New King James Version)

⁸ Again, the _____ took Him up on an exceedingly high _____, and showed Him all the _____ of the world and their _____. ⁹ And he said to Him, "All these things I will give You if You will _____ _____ and _____ _____."

*¹⁰ Then _____ said to him, "Away with you,[d] Satan! For it is _____, 'You shall _____ the L*ORD *your God, and Him only you shall _____.'"[e]*

¹¹ Then the devil left Him, and behold, _____ came and _____ to Him.

Day 43

Jeremiah 29 (New King James Version)

¹¹ For I know the thoughts that I think toward you, says the LORD, thoughts of peace and not of evil, to give you a future and a hope. ¹² Then you will call upon Me and go and pray to Me, and I will listen to you. ¹³ And you will seek Me and find Me, when you search for Me with all your heart. ¹⁴ I will be found by you, says the LORD, and I will bring you back from your captivity; I will gather you from all the nations and from all the places where I have driven you, says the LORD, and I will bring you to the place from which I cause you to be carried away captive.

If you trust in the Lord he will provide for you.

After reading this scripture I think...

_____

_____

_____

_____

_____

The Lord has provided me a future, so what I need to do is....

_____

_____

_____

_____

_____

We are one big family, doesn't matter if you like it or agree with it. We are many nations because of God's plan and we will eventually be one nation because it is God's plan. Being a member of this nation, who's only purpose is to worship the Lord, is based on how you worship Him now. How can what you have or how much you make impress a God who provided those things for you? Don't be fooled by the things of this world, seek the Lord with all your heart.

Day 44

Malachi 2 (New King James Version)

¹⁰ Have we not all one Father?
Has not one God created us?
Why do we deal treacherously with one another
By profaning the covenant of the fathers?

We are from one father and I treat everyone like…..

_____
_____
_____
_____

We were created by one God but we have allowed…

_____
_____
_____
_____

Day 45

Do you know the names of Jesus Christ?

```
L J A E S T U H E S L C
H U R G S I S A M T O I
S G F I E O D V M A R S
L J R R G M U O A H D A
J H E W E O O H N P L V
C I O S F D D E U L G I
N R Z A U R N J E A Q O
D E M B S S G O L E C R
Z E G V G K R N W X P Z
N G H D H Q F E I A E W
V K I R T Z X L F K L Y
C J B E H A I S S E M J
```

AMEN   **ALPHA**
CHRIST   **SAVIOR**
EMMANUEL   **WONDERFUL**
GOD   **WORD**
JEHOVAH   **KING**
JESUS   **LORD**
OMEGA   **MESSIAH**

Day 46

Isaiah 1 (New King James Version)

¹⁸ *"Come now, and let us reason together,"*
Says the L<small>ORD</small>,
"Though your sins are like scarlet,
They shall be as white as snow;
Though they are red like crimson,
They shall be as wool.
¹⁹ *If you are willing and obedient,*
You shall eat the good of the land;
²⁰ *But if you refuse and rebel,*
You shall be devoured by the sword";
For the mouth of the L<small>ORD</small> has spoken.

Match the items below

1. The wealthiest king
2. Number of Books of the Bible
3. Sodom and
4. Abraham's companion
5. Bible Version
6. Number of plagues Moses presented to Pharaoh
7. Compassion from Samaria
8. Number of Disciples

A. 66
B. 12
C. Good Samaritan
D. Solomon
E. Aaron
F. 10
G. Gomorrah
H. New King James

Day 47

Matthew 20 (New King James Version)

29 Now as they went out of Jericho, a great multitude followed Him. 30 And behold, two blind men sitting by the road, when they heard that Jesus was passing by, cried out, saying, "Have mercy on us, O Lord, Son of David!"

31 Then the multitude warned them that they should be quiet; but they cried out all the more, saying, "Have mercy on us, O Lord, Son of David!"

32 So Jesus stood still and called them, and said, "What do you want Me to do for you?"

33 They said to Him, "Lord, that our eyes may be opened." 34 So Jesus had compassion and touched their eyes. And immediately their eyes received sight, and they followed Him

This scripture pertains to two men who could not see and asked Jesus to give them sight. We, although we have sight, should maybe ask Jesus to allow us to see things with spiritual sight. When we can physically see how something can work out we loose faith and doubt it can ever happen. This is because we are using just our eyes and not our heart. We know that Jesus is not limited by what we see but limited by what we believe. With that being said, how good is your vision?

After reading this I believe…

_____
_____
_____
_____
_____
_____
_____
_____

Day 48

Romans 3 (New King James Version)

^{10} As it is written:

"There is none righteous, no, not one;
^{11} There is none who understands;
There is none who seeks after God.
^{12} They have all turned aside;
They have together become unprofitable;
There is none who does good, no, not one."[b]
^{13} "Their throat is an open tomb;
With their tongues they have practiced deceit"; [c]
"The poison of asps is under their lips"; [d]
^{14} "Whose mouth is full of cursing and bitterness."[e]
^{15} "Their feet are swift to shed blood;
^{16} Destruction and misery are in their ways;
^{17} And the way of peace they have not known."[f]
^{18} "There is no fear of God before their eyes."[g]

Myths and Misunderstandings

Although I still sin, I know I'm not as bad as some other people

My mother and my grandmother was saved, so I know I'm going to heaven

I only lie if it benefits me, so that's not really being a liar

I don't pay my tithes every time I get paid but I give some to charity so it evens out

Looking at women is just what men do, it's nothing wrong with it

Flirting with married men is harmless and accepting gifts is okay too

Day 49

Deuteronomy 18 (New King James Version)

⁹ "When you come into the land which the LORD your God is giving you, you shall not learn to follow the abominations of those nations. ¹⁰ There shall not be found among you anyone who makes his son or his daughter pass through the fire, or one who practices witchcraft, or a soothsayer, or one who interprets omens, or a sorcerer, ¹¹ or one who conjures spells, or a medium, or a spiritist, or one who calls up the dead. ¹² For all who do these things are an abomination to the LORD, and because of these abominations the LORD your God drives them out from before you. ¹³ You shall be blameless before the LORD your God. ¹⁴ For these nations which you will dispossess listened to soothsayers and diviners; but as for you, the LORD your God has not appointed such for you.

When I read this I thing about…

_____

_____

_____

_____

_____

This land is filled with people who try to convince me to do certain things, so I….

_____

_____

_____

_____

_____

Day 50

Matthew 22 (New King James Version)

[34] But when the Pharisees heard that He had silenced the Sadducees, they gathered together. [35] Then one of them, a lawyer, asked Him a question, testing Him, and saying, [36] "Teacher, which is the great commandment in the law?"

[37] Jesus said to him, "'You shall love the LORD your God with all your heart, with all your soul, and with all your mind.'[d] [38] This is the first and great commandment. [39] And the second is like it: 'You shall love your neighbor as yourself.'[e] [40] On these two commandments hang all the Law and the Prophets."

Is this a commandment you practice daily?

Yes and…

_____
_____
_____
_____

No and…

_____
_____
_____
_____

Rewrite the commandments here

You_____
_____

This is the first and great commandment.

And the second

You_____
_____

On these two commandments hang all the Law and the Prophets

Day 51

Ephesians 1 (New King James Version)

³ Blessed be the God and Father of our Lord Jesus Christ, who has blessed us with every spiritual blessing in the heavenly places in Christ, ⁴ just as He chose us in Him before the foundation of the world, that we should be holy and without blame before Him in love, ⁵ having predestined us to adoption as sons by Jesus Christ to Himself, according to the good pleasure of His will, ⁶ to the praise of the glory of His grace, by which He made us accepted in the Beloved.

⁷ In Him we have redemption through His blood, the forgiveness of sins, according to the riches of His grace ⁸ which He made to abound toward us in all wisdom and prudence, ⁹ having made known to us the mystery of His will, according to His good pleasure which He purposed in Himself, ¹⁰ that in the dispensation of the fullness of the times He might gather together in one all things in Christ, both[a] which are in heaven and which are on earth—in Him. ¹¹ In Him also we have obtained an inheritance, being predestined according to the purpose of Him who works all things according to the counsel of His will, ¹² that we who first trusted in Christ should be to the praise of His glory.

¹³ In Him you also trusted, after you heard the word of truth, the gospel of your salvation; in whom also, having believed, you were sealed with the Holy Spirit of promise, ¹⁴ who[b] is the guarantee of our inheritance until the redemption of the purchased possession, to the praise of His glory.

No questions, nothing to write………Just read, believe and share this good news.

God bless you on this day.

Day 52

1 John 3 (New King James Version)

18 My little children, let us not love in word or in tongue, but in deed and in truth.

It is very important to keep God's words with you daily, so that we may *act* out the love we *say* we have.

Here are a few books that may help you in your Christian walk.

1. **The Purpose Drive Life**. By: Dr. Rick Warren
2. **Every Single Man's Battle**. By Stephen Arterburn & Fred Stoeker (this series also contains Every Married Man's, Single woman's and Married Women's battle)
3. **A.S.K: Unleashing the Power of Prayer**. By: Dr. Jack Graham
4. **I Love You, However**. By: Andy Bethea
5. **Sleeping Giants**. By: Bishop T.D. Jakes (dvd)
6. **Your Best Life Now**. By: Joel Osteen

There are so many ways to keep Satan from steeling the life out of you each morning. I know you may not have time to read each morning but there are other options.

- Make an inspirational CD to listen to as you get dressed and drive to work.
- Have the T.V on something to inspire you as you begin your day.
- Be sure to speak with a trusted friend and a true believer each morning. This will help you both.
- Identify what Satan is using to get you off your path and confront that issue (this does not mean going to work and telling off your boss) It means when you know what is bothering you, you should be able to deal with it better
- Check yourself to make sure you aren't the one steeling the life out of others (yes Satan can use you too)
- **BEGIN EACH DAY WITH PRAYER, REGARDLESS OF HOW YOU FEEL OR WHAT YOU MAY BE FACING.**

Day 53

Matthew 4 (New King James Version)

[19] Then He said to them, "Follow Me, and I will make you fishers of men." [20] They immediately left their nets and followed Him.

My wife and I were listening to Pastor Mike Jones on our way to Maryland. He said "How you bait your hook, determines what you catch". I immediately began thinking about how people attract mates and friends. How they obtain jobs or progress through life.

1. Did you use short skirts and low cut tops to catch your husband?
2. Did you buy things for your wife and her friends to impress her when you were trying to catch her?
3. Did you flirt or maybe even sleep with someone to get a promotion or get a job?
4. Did you begin your present relationship cheating with this person and now you are with them and don't trust them.
5. Did you lie, cheat and steel to open your own business that is now going bankrupt?

When you use lies, deceit and bad intentions as bait, why wouldn't you expect to catch liars, cheaters and people with bad intentions?

1. I have tried to keep my old friends but also surround myself with new friends that are deeply rooted in Christ.   True [ ]   False [ ]

2. If, after reading this, I have to choose between being honest or not being honest to get a promotion or a better job, I will _____.

3. I now know that as a "Fisher of Men" my behavior could determine what I catch and the ones that get away. So I plan to….

_____
_____
_____
_____

Day 54

2 Timothy 1 (New King James Version)

[7] For God has not given us a spirit of fear, but of power and of love and of a sound mind.

We usually fear that which we do not understand. People who fear the end of the world are people who do not understand God or His word. Being well versed in what the Bible tells us may not prevent you from ever being afraid again but it can better prepare you in dealing with those fears.

1. I usually fear _____
   but once I _____ I feel
   much better.
2. When I hear people predicting the end of the world I _____
   because I understand that _____.
3. Having fear is also a lack of faith, I _____
   To increase my faith and reduce the things I fear.
4. Having a sound mind should produce better decisions. Before I rush into anything
   I _____ and talk to _____.
5. Sometimes our fears can stem from our lack of confidence in ourselves. However, having the power and love provided by God should increase that confidence. Maybe if I

   _____
   _____
   _____
   _____

   I would feel better about me, my decisions and my ability to accomplish things.

Day 55

ACROSS

1 Shampoo brand
6 Agency (abbr.)
10 Craft
14 Relating to birds
15 Card game
16 Garbed
17 Trial
19 Tease
20 Deleted
21 Nothing
23 Hobo
24 Attack
26 Mexican drink
28 Resort hotel
31 Aurora
33 Move quickly
34 Wheeled vehicle
35 Berried shrub
37 Objects
41 Comparable
43 Time period
44 Navigation system
45 Boyfriends
46 Florida City
48 Past
59 Atmosphere
60 Ballet skirt
62 She was too busy with chores
67 Supplication
69 Acknowledgment ofsins
71 Was looked at
72 Musical repeat
73 Happening
74 Whirl
75 Aroma
76 Bout

DOWN

1 Opp. of love
2 Declare
3 Capital of Peru
4 Dupes
5 Bets
6 American Federation of Teachers (abbr.)
7 Get
8 Someone from Croatia
9 Over there (KJV)
10 Metric weight unit
11 Defense
12 Capital of Afghanistan
49 Insult
51 She
52 Bro. or sis.
53 John the Baptist ate them
13 Water retention
18 Bye
22 Husband of Priscilla
25 Celestial "tailed" body
27 Do ___ others
28 Replace a striker
29 Pallid
30 Opera solo
32 Wife of Abraham
35 Chauvinist
57 Liberal (abbr.)
36 Hard to pass through a needle?
38 Epochs
39 They brought gifts
40 Stuck up person
42 Antelope
47 Undercoat
50 Plaster
53 Regress
54 Lubricated
55 Statement of beliefs
56 Arose
58 Baseball plates
61 Reverse
63 Invitation abbreviation
64 Level
65 Polish
66 Stake
68 Some
70 Further

Puzzle provided by: Christian Bible Reference Site – Cliff Leitch

Day 56

Complete the following scriptures

Ephesians 2 (New King James Version)

⁴ But God, who is _____ in mercy, because of His great _____ with which He loved us, ⁵ even when we were dead in _____, made us alive together with Christ (by _____ you have been _____), ⁶ and raised us up together, and made us sit together in the _____ places in Christ Jesus, ⁷ that in the ages to come He might show the _____ _____ of His grace in His kindness toward us in Christ Jesus. ⁸ For by _____ you have been saved through _____, and that not of yourselves; it is the _____ of God, ⁹ not of works, lest anyone should _____. ¹⁰ For we are His workmanship, created in Christ Jesus for good works, which God prepared beforehand that we should walk in them.

1 Timothy 6 (New King James Version)

³ If anyone teaches _____ and does not consent to _____ words, even the words of our Lord Jesus Christ, and to the _____ which accords with godliness, ⁴ he is proud, knowing nothing, but is _____ with disputes and arguments over words, from which come _____, strife, reviling, evil suspicions, ⁵ useless wranglings[a] of men of _____ minds and destitute of the truth, who suppose that godliness is a means of gain. From such_____ yourself.[b]

Day 57

Psalm 95 (New King James Version)

Oh come, let us sing to the LORD!
Let us shout joyfully to the Rock of our salvation.
² Let us come before His presence with thanksgiving;
Let us shout joyfully to Him with psalms.
³ For the LORD is the great God,
And the great King above all gods.
⁴ In His hand are the deep places of the earth;
The heights of the hills are His also.
⁵ The sea is His, for He made it;
And His hands formed the dry land.

3 John 1 (New King James Version)

[11] Beloved, do not imitate what is evil, but what is good. He who does good is of God, but[d] he who does evil has not seen God.

Deuteronomy 13 (New King James Version)

If there arises among you a prophet or a dreamer of dreams, and he gives you a sign or a wonder, ² and the sign or the wonder comes to pass, of which he spoke to you, saying, 'Let us go after other gods'—which you have not known—'and let us serve them,' ³ you shall not listen to the words of that prophet or that dreamer of dreams, for the LORD your God is testing you to know whether you love the LORD your God with all your heart and with all your soul. ⁴ You shall walk after the LORD your God and fear Him, and keep His commandments and obey His voice; you shall serve Him and hold fast to Him.

Having directions will keep you from getting lost

Day 58

Daniel 2 (New King James Version)

20 Daniel answered and said:

"Blessed be the name of God forever and ever,
For wisdom and might are His.
21 And He changes the times and the seasons;
He removes kings and raises up kings;
He gives wisdom to the wise
And knowledge to those who have understanding.
22 He reveals deep and secret things;
He knows what is in the darkness,
And light dwells with Him.

23 "I thank You and praise You,
O God of my fathers;
You have given me wisdom and might,
And have now made known to me what we asked of You,
For You have made known to us the king's demand."

My thoughts about this scripture

_____
_____
_____
_____
_____

Do you believe that God gives us things while we sleep?

_____
_____
_____

Day 59

Matthew 2 (New King James Version)

13 Now when they had departed, behold, an angel of the Lord appeared to Joseph in a dream, saying, "Arise, take the young Child and His mother, flee to Egypt, and stay there until I bring you word; for Herod will seek the young Child to destroy Him."

14 When he arose, he took the young Child and His mother by night and departed for Egypt, 15 and was there until the death of Herod, that it might be fulfilled which was spoken by the Lord through the prophet, saying, "Out of Egypt I called My Son."[b]

1. Do you believe that when things happen in your life, good or bad, it is to fulfill things that God has already spoken for your life?
2. After reading this, do you feel it is okay to "flee" sometimes instead of always fighting?

My thoughts about this scripture..

_____
_____
_____
_____
_____

Day 60

Matthew 6 (New King James Version)

"Moreover, when you fast, do not be like the hypocrites, with a sad countenance. For they disfigure their faces that they may appear to men to be fasting. Assuredly, I say to you, they have their reward. [17] But you, when you fast, anoint your head and wash your face, [18] so that you do not appear to men to be fasting, but to your Father who is in the secret place; and your Father who sees in secret will reward you openly.[d]

Fasting - is primarily the act of willingly abstaining from some or all food, drink, or both, for a period of time

Fasting - is the most powerful spiritual discipline of all the Christian disciplines. Through fasting and prayer, the Holy Spirit can transform your life.

The idea of fasting is to give up something that you really enjoy. However, there has to be an effort to move closer to Christ during this time as well. You should replace those things you're giving up with God's word.

When I fast I..

_____
_____
_____

I have not attempted a fast because.

_____
_____
_____

Day 61

Exodus 36 (New International Version)

¹ So Bezalel, Oholiab and every skilled person to whom the LORD has given skill and ability to know how to carry out all the work of constructing the sanctuary are to do the work just as the LORD has commanded."

² Then Moses summoned Bezalel and Oholiab and every skilled person to whom the LORD had given ability and who was willing to come and do the work. ³ They received from Moses all the offerings the Israelites had brought to carry out the work of constructing the sanctuary. And the people continued to bring freewill offerings morning after morning. ⁴ So all the skilled workers who were doing all the work on the sanctuary left what they were doing ⁵ and said to Moses, "The people are bringing more than enough for doing the work the LORD commanded to be done."

⁶ Then Moses gave an order and they sent this word throughout the camp: "No man or woman is to make anything else as an offering for the sanctuary." And so the people were restrained from bringing more, ⁷ because what they already had was more than enough to do all the work.

So many things come to mind when I read this.

First, did you see how when everyone comes together, doing their part to build a sanctuary and it is done as God commands, your resources are endless? These people didn't just pay tithes and hope for the best. They gave according to what was most important to them. I challenge you to find any church that has recently asked its members to stop giving because they had already done more than enough.

My thoughts about this scripture..

_____
_____
_____
_____
_____

Day 62

Psalm 73 (New King James Version)

Truly God is good to Israel,
To such as are pure in heart.
² But as for me, my feet had almost stumbled;
My steps had nearly slipped.
³ For I was envious of the boastful,
When I saw the prosperity of the wicked.

⁴ For there are no pangs in their death,
But their strength is firm.
⁵ They are not in trouble as other men,
Nor are they plagued like other men.
⁶ Therefore pride serves as their necklace;
Violence covers them like a garment.
⁷ Their eyes bulge[a] with abundance;
They have more than heart could wish.
⁸ They scoff and speak wickedly concerning oppression;
They speak loftily.
⁹ They set their mouth against the heavens,
And their tongue walks through the earth.

Most people who brag and boast about what they have or what they have accomplished are people who usually don't give God enough credit. If you truly understand that you may accumulate things as a non-believer but those things will never give you the peace and joy that comes from God.

1. I don't boast about anything because I know…

   _____
   _____
   _____

2. I usually listen to people talking about what they have and I …

   _____
   _____
   _____

Day 63

Acts 3 (New King James Version)

3 Now Peter and John went up together to the temple at the hour of prayer, the ninth hour. ² And a certain man lame from his mother's womb was carried, whom they laid daily at the gate of the temple which is called Beautiful, to ask alms from those who entered the temple; ³ who, seeing Peter and John about to go into the temple, asked for alms. ⁴ And fixing his eyes on him, with John, Peter said, "Look at us." ⁵ So he gave them his attention, expecting to receive something from them. ⁶ Then Peter said, "Silver and gold I do not have, but what I do have I give you: In the name of Jesus Christ of Nazareth, rise up and walk." ⁷ And he took him by the right hand and lifted him up, and immediately his feet and ankle bones received strength. ⁸ So he, leaping up, stood and walked and entered the temple with them—walking, leaping, and praising God. ⁹ And all the people saw him walking and praising God. ¹⁰ Then they knew that it was he who sat begging alms at the Beautiful Gate of the temple; and they were filled with wonder and amazement at what had happened to him.

When I read this scripture I..

_____

When you picture the man walking, leaping and praising God, does it make you wonder why we spend so much time asking for "silver & gold" and not God's blessings?

_____

Day 64

1 John 4 (New King James Version)

Beloved, do not believe every spirit, but test the spirits, whether they are of God; because many false prophets have gone out into the world. ² By this you know the Spirit of God: Every spirit that confesses that Jesus Christ has come in the flesh is of God, ³ and every spirit that does not confess that[a] Jesus Christ has come in the flesh is not of God. And this is the spirit of the Antichrist, which you have heard was coming, and is now already in the world.

1. I believe anything as long as the word "God" or "Jesus" is in it.
   [ ] True   [ ] False

2. I may not know God's voice but I am sure that if something is telling me to do wrong, it is not from God.
   [ ] True   [ ] False

3. I try to be sure I know God's word so I am not easily persuaded
   [ ] True   [ ] False

After reading this scripture I…

_____

_____

_____

_____

_____

Day 65

Job 23 (New King James Version)

But He knows the way that I take;
When He has tested me, I shall come forth as gold.
[11] My foot has held fast to His steps;
I have kept His way and not turned aside.
[12] I have not departed from the commandment of His lips;
I have treasured the words of His mouth
More than my necessary food.

Denise was a substitute teacher for a local elementary school. On Wednesdays and Thursdays she volunteers at her church. Her duties were filing, typing and keeping things organized. She covers for the receptionist during her lunch break and sometimes even helps prepare for Bible study. One afternoon Denise was making copies and the machine needed paper. On her way to the supply room she passed the office of the church treasurer. She could hear her on the phone and Denise heard her mention her name. *"Denise works here two days a week and you would think she owns the place. Everything has to be just right for little Ms. Perfect",* the treasurer added.

Denise couldn't believe her ears. She reached for the door with the intent of confronting the lady but something stopped her. She heard a soft voice saying to her, *"If you tend to what I have asked of you, I will tend to those who oppose you".* Denise smiled and continued on to the supply room.

After about an hour, the Pastor came into an office where Denise was working. He spoke to her and asked about the flyers he asked her to print for him. *"They look great!"* he said. *"But why am I surprised, you always do a great job",* he added. She thanked him and as the two continued to talk the treasurer walked in. The Pastor showed her the flyers Denise made. *"Those are beautiful. Denise, girl you really have an eye for detail".* *"Thank you",* Denise replied. She placed the flyer on the desk and walked over to Denise and hugged her. Denise, without hesitation, hugged her back.

Denise left the church with the understanding that she was being tested. God gave her direction to let it go and allow him to handle it. Although it was very difficult not saying anything to the lady, Denise knew that confronting her would be self gratifying for a short period of time but following God's direction would satisfy her for life.

Day 66

Find these verses and write them below.

1. Exodus 3:1-3 (New King James Version)

_____
_____
_____
_____
_____
_____

2. Deuteronomy 23: 19-20 (New King James Version)

_____
_____
_____
_____
_____
_____

3. Philippians 2 (New King James Version)

_____
_____
_____
_____
_____
_____

Day 67

Find these verses and write them below

4. 2:7-11 Corinthians 10 (New King James Version)

_____
_____
_____
_____
_____
_____
_____

5. 2:18-19 Chronicles 20 (New King James Version)

_____
_____
_____
_____
_____
_____

3. John 3:16-17 (New King James Version)

_____
_____
_____
_____
_____
_____

Day 68

Hosea 6 (New King James Version)

Come, and let us return to the LORD;
For He has torn, but He will heal us;
He has stricken, but He will bind us up.
² After two days He will revive us;
On the third day He will raise us up,
That we may live in His sight.
³ Let us know,
Let us pursue the knowledge of the LORD.
His going forth is established as the morning;
He will come to us like the rain,
Like the latter and former rain to the earth.

What I think about this scripture.

_____
_____
_____
_____

Having faith that God will lift you up is..

_____
_____
_____
_____

Day 69

Luke 1 (New King James Version)

[39] Now Mary arose in those days and went into the hill country with haste, to a city of Judah, [40] and entered the house of Zacharias and greeted Elizabeth. [41] And it happened, when Elizabeth heard the greeting of Mary, that the babe leaped in her womb; and Elizabeth was filled with the Holy Spirit. [42] Then she spoke out with a loud voice and said, "Blessed are you among women, and blessed is the fruit of your womb! [43] But why is this granted to me, that the mother of my Lord should come to me? [44] For indeed, as soon as the voice of your greeting sounded in my ears, the babe leaped in my womb for joy. [45] Blessed is she who believed, for there will be a fulfillment of those things which were told her from the Lord.

Some scripture is inspiring each time you read it.

When I read this I..

_____

_____

_____

_____

_____

_____

Day 70

Exodus 18 (New King James Version)

15 And Moses said to his father-in-law, "Because the people come to me to inquire of God. 16 When they have a difficulty, they come to me, and I judge between one and another; and I make known the statutes of God and His laws."

17 So Moses' father-in-law said to him, "The thing that you do is not good. 18 Both you and these people who are with you will surely wear yourselves out. For this thing is too much for you; you are not able to perform it by yourself. 19 Listen now to my voice; I will give you counsel, and God will be with you: Stand before God for the people, so that you may bring the difficulties to God. 20 And you shall teach them the statutes and the laws, and show them the way in which they must walk and the work they must do. 21 Moreover you shall select from all the people able men, such as fear God, men of truth, hating covetousness; and place such over them to be rulers of thousands, rulers of hundreds, rulers of fifties, and rulers of tens. 22 And let them judge the people at all times. Then it will be that every great matter they shall bring to you, but every small matter they themselves shall judge. So it will be easier for you, for they will bear the burden with you. 23 If you do this thing, and God so commands you, then you will be able to endure, and all this people will also go to their place in peace."

Although the Bible does not say this or even suggest it, this sounds like the forming of what a church should be. All issues of the congregation should not fall on the shoulders of the Pastor. There should be trusted workers in every church willing to help carry this load.

1. Do you have a role at your church?
2. Are you willing to assist others when they have issues?
3. If you are a true believer and you have leadership qualities, have you offered those services to your pastor?
4. Do you feel that every issue you have is so important it can only be heard by the Pastor?
5. Are you so saved and sanctified that you feel only the Pastor is important enough to help you?

Day 71

Finish the following;

Leviticus 1 (New King James Version)

Now the LORD called to Moses, and spoke to him from the tabernacle of meeting, saying,

_____
_____
_____
_____

Job 2 (New King James Version)

³ Then the LORD said to Satan, "Have you considered My servant Job,

_____
_____
_____
_____

1 Peter 2 (New King James Version)

⁹ But you are a chosen generation

_____
_____

¹⁰ who once were

_____
_____
_____

Day 72

1. The Bible consists of;

    A. New Testament & Old Testament
    B. 66 Books
    C. Letters written by John
    D. All of the above

2. Give four other names for Jesus

    A.
    B.
    C.
    D.

3. Name "The Twelve"

    1.   7.
    2.   8.
    3.   9.
    4.   10.
    5.   11.
    6.   12.

4. _____ is the first book of the Bible and _____ is the last.

5. _____ kissed Jesus on the check when the guards came to arrest Him.

6. Name the job of one of the twelve before being chosen by Jesus.
_____ was a _____ .

Day 73

Matthew 10 (New King James Version)

⁵ These twelve Jesus sent out and commanded them, saying: "Do not go into the way of the Gentiles, and do not enter a city of the Samaritans. ⁶ But go rather to the lost sheep of the house of Israel. ⁷ And as you go, preach, saying, 'The kingdom of heaven is at hand.' ⁸ Heal the sick, cleanse the lepers, raise the dead,[c] cast out demons. Freely you have received, freely give. ⁹ Provide neither gold nor silver nor copper in your money belts, ¹⁰ nor bag for your journey, nor two tunics, nor sandals, nor staffs; for a worker is worthy of his food.

¹¹ "Now whatever city or town you enter, inquire who in it is worthy, and stay there till you go out. ¹² And when you go into a household, greet it. ¹³ If the household is worthy, let your peace come upon it. But if it is not worthy, let your peace return to you. ¹⁴ And whoever will not receive you nor hear your words, when you depart from that house or city, shake off the dust from your feet. ¹⁵ Assuredly, I say to you, it will be more tolerable for the land of Sodom and Gomorrah in the day of judgment than for that city!

What I think when I read this scripture

_____
_____
_____
_____

God has chosen others to preach since "The Twelve", do you feel people are called to preach?

_____
_____
_____
_____

Day 74

Proverbs

1. The Book of Proverbs has _____ chapters.
A. 27
B. 46
C. 31
D. 17

2. King Solomon was the son of _____.
A. Job
B. David
C. Moses
D. Jesus

3. Proverbs 3:9 says;
A. Honor the Lord with your possessions and with the first fruits of all your increase.
B. Do not enter the path of the wicked, and do not walk in the way of evil.
C. For God so loved the world that He gave His only begotten son.
D. That every man should set free his male and female slave.

4. After you locate the correct answer to number three tell where the other scriptures came from.

_____

_____
_____
_____
_____

Day 75

Complete the following;

Ruth 2 (New King James Version)

1. *There was a relative of_____ husband, a man of great wealth, of the family of_____. His name was_____.* [2] *So Ruth the Moabitess said to Naomi, "Please let me _____, and glean heads of grain after him in whose sight I may find favor*

Ruth 3 (New King James Version)

2. [8] *Now it happened at _____ that the man was startled, and turned himself; and there, a woman was _____.* [9] *And he said, "Who are you?"So she answered, "I am_____, your _____. Take your maidservant under your wing,[a] for you are a close relative."*

Ruth 4 (New King James Version)

3. [13] *So Boaz took Ruth and she became_____; and when he went in to her, the LORD gave her conception, and she bore a _____.* [14] *Then the women said to Naomi, "_____, who has not left you this day without a close relative; and may his name be famous in _____!* [15] *And may he be to you a restorer of life and a_____ of your old age; for your daughter-in-law, who loves you, who is better to you than seven sons, has borne him."* [16] *Then _____took the child and laid him on her bosom, and became a nurse to him.* [17] *Also the neighbor women gave him a name, saying, "There is a son born to Naomi." And they called his name_____. He is the father of_____, the father of _____.*

Day 76

FMBC

```
P  U  O  G  W  F  I  G  E  L  B  I  B  I  V
U  I  U  U  A  K  N  M  N  R  W  D  P  I  J
M  M  H  M  T  I  C  E  N  T  E  R  E  D  C
O  I  I  S  S  S  O  E  C  F  G  B  R  H
T  L  C  I  D  U  Z  R  U  G  H  N  Z  I  R
Y  Y  A  L  S  N  O  N  U  X  J  I  O  L  I
C  R  T  E  V  S  E  I  I  S  L  H  R  U  S
P  Z  J  V  E  W  E  I  Y  D  U  C  Q  S  T
H  W  T  P  H  H  G  T  R  V  W  A  C  U  T
I  L  O  V  E  Q  E  S  O  F  M  E  W  U  L
D  Y  X  V  Z  G  J  O  L  R  B  R  P  D  O
R  E  B  Z  J  O  P  X  G  J  O  F  V  Q  T
Q  N  S  S  H  B  S  G  T  T  J  Z  J  N  L
E  C  U  A  K  Y  B  O  Q  C  G  Z  N  G  P
S  D  Y  A  B  H  D  E  Z  Q  Q  H  D  C  T
```

BASED	BIBLE	CENTERED
CHIRST	CHRIST	FAMILY
FRIENDSHIP	GLORY	JESUS
LOVE	OUT	PRAISING
REACHING		

Day 77

Isaiah 55 (New King James Version)

[8] "For My thoughts are not your thoughts,
Nor are your ways My ways," says the LORD.
[9] "For as the heavens are higher than the earth,
So are My ways higher than your ways,
And My thoughts than your thoughts.

We sometimes convince ourselves that we think as God thinks. We believe we can "help him out" by making decisions on our own. Usually it is when the decision best benefits what we want. Even on our best days we don't come close to thinking on God's level. Although you may have done something a thousand times, still seeks God's advice before doing it again.

About this scripture

_____
_____
_____
_____

When it comes to major decisions I still seek Gods advice, even if it is something I've done before.

Yes

_____
_____
_____

No

_____
_____
_____

Both Yes and No

_____
_____
_____
_____

The Book of Matthew

1. John was also known as
A. John the Healer
B. John the Preacher
C. John the Baptist
D. John of Galilee

2. Jesus was led into the wilderness to be tempted by
    A. The Priest
    B. The Devil
    C. The Pharaoh
    D. The Gentiles

3. It is said that "If your right eye causes you to sin" you should
    A. Pluck it out and cast it from you
    B. Use an eye patch
    C. Walk with your head down
    D. Not make eye contact to avoid lust

4. Jesus tells us not to worry about three things, they are
    A. What you will eat, drink or wear
    B. What you will buy, sell or trade
    C. What you will pray, sing or praise
    D. What you will, eat, pray or dream

Day 79

Hebrews 11 (New King James Version)

Now faith is the substance of things hoped for, the evidence of things not seen. [2] *For by it the elders obtained a good testimony.*

[3] *By faith we understand that the worlds were framed by the word of God, so that the things which are seen were not made of things which are visible.*

What I understand from this is..

_____
_____
_____
_____

My faith is..

_____
_____
_____
_____

My faith lacks..

_____
_____
_____
_____

Day 80

Deuteronomy 26 (New King James Version)

14 I have not eaten any of it when in mourning, nor have I removed any of it for an unclean use, nor given any of it for the dead. I have obeyed the voice of the LORD my God, and have done according to all that You have commanded me. 15 Look down from Your holy habitation, from heaven, and bless Your people Israel and the land which You have given us, just as You swore to our fathers, "a land flowing with milk and honey."'[d]

Being obedient is hard but I..

_____
_____
_____
_____
_____

Knowing God made a promise to our fathers makes me….

_____
_____
_____
_____
_____

Just because the promise was made I still understand I must…

_____
_____
_____
_____
_____

Day 81

To show God how much I love him, today I will….

_____
_____

Although I have a co-worker/friend who gets me off track, today I will…

_____
_____
_____
_____

Today I will be honest about everything. I will not lie for personal gain. And…

_____
_____

Today I will not speak poorly about anyone, jump to conclusions or be rude because things are not going my way. And…..

_____
_____

Today I will thank God several times during the day because without Him I could not have accomplished anything. And…..

_____
_____

Today I will begin my journey the way the Lord intended me to. And…..

_____
_____

Today, not tomorrow, my life will begin to change for the better because I am going to change. And…..

_____
_____

Today I finally understand that I am a child of God and my father is there for me. And…

_____
_____

Day 82

Joshua 1 (New King James Version)

⁵ No man shall be able to stand before you all the days of your life; as I was with Moses, so I will be with you. I will not leave you nor forsake you. ⁶ Be strong and of good courage, for to this people you shall divide as an inheritance the land which I swore to their fathers to give them. ⁷ Only be strong and very courageous, that you may observe to do according to all the law which Moses My servant commanded you; do not turn from it to the right hand or to the left, that you may prosper wherever you go. ⁸ This Book of the Law shall not depart from your mouth, but you shall meditate in it day and night, that you may observe to do according to all that is written in it. For then you will make your way prosperous, and then you will have good success. ⁹ Have I not commanded you? Be strong and of good courage; do not be afraid, nor be dismayed, for the LORD your God is with you wherever you go."

1. If God tells us that if we follow His word we will prosper in whatever we do, why are we so afraid to try things?

   _____
   _____
   _____

2. God has commanded us to "Be strong and of good courage", yet we fear everything. What does that say about our faith in Christ?

   _____
   _____
   _____

3. The Book of the Law not only tells us what we should be doing, it also tells us what we are entitled to by doing those things. Is this also why God says we should meditate in it day and night?

   _____
   _____
   _____

Day 83

Steven was recently hired as a manager for a convenience store. Although he was hired to cover the overnight shift, he was happy to have a job after being without one for about six months. Steven arrived to work early and worked as long as it took to ensure everything was ready for the next shift. He not only had a new job but he also had a new woman in his life, Paula. Paula worked in a retail store, about the same hours as Steven so the hours didn't cause issues in their social lives. Paula was also a strong believer in Christ where as Steven believed, he just didn't pursue the Lord the way she did.

As their relationship grew stronger, so did Steven's relationship with Christ. They began attending church together, they attended Bible study together. Steven even joined the men's choir. Things were going great for them in church and at work.

One afternoon when Steven arrived at work, his supervisor asked to speak with him. He told Steven how impressed he was with his work and asked if he would be interested in managing his own store. Steven was excited about the opportunity. His manager explained that it was not definite but he would mention his name in the next meeting as a possible replacement for the retiring manager. He mentioned that he would need to update his resume' and references.

Steven went home after work and called Paula to share the news. Paula was excited for him and offered to help him with his resume'. Steven suddenly remembered that when he completed his resume' for his present position, he wasn't completely honest with all his information. Of course he was not living a Christian life during that time and it did not bother him as much as it does now. Furthermore, he would have to tell those same lies again to obtain this job and possible to keep his present one.

Steven explained the situation to Paula and asked how he should handle it. Paula told him the decision had to be his but to consider what is more important to him, a job or his relationship with God. Without hesitation Steven called his manager and explained the situation to him.

**What happened afterwards is not as important as the decision he made.
What's more important to you?**

Day 84

Jonah 3 (New King James Version)

⁵ So the people of Nineveh believed God, proclaimed a fast, and put on sackcloth, from the greatest to the least of them. ⁶ Then word came to the king of Nineveh; and he arose from his throne and laid aside his robe, covered himself with sackcloth and sat in ashes. ⁷ And he caused it to be proclaimed and published throughout Nineveh by the decree of the king and his nobles, saying,

Let neither man nor beast, herd nor flock, taste anything; do not let them eat, or drink water. ⁸ But let man and beast be covered with sackcloth, and cry mightily to God; yes, let every one turn from his evil way and from the violence that is in his hands. ⁹ Who can tell if God will turn and relent, and turn away from His fierce anger, so that we may not perish?

¹⁰ Then God saw their works, that they turned from their evil way; and God relented from the disaster that He had said He would bring upon them, and He did not do it.

1. Do you still need to be reminded that what you're doing could lead to disaster?
   _____
   _____

2. What does it take for you to humble yourself?
   _____
   _____

3. How often do you feel you can do the same things that are not pleasing to God as long as you say you are sorry?
   _____
   _____

   My thoughts about this scripture..
   _____
   _____
   _____
   _____
   _____
   _____

Day 85

Give your honest response to the following. After 3 months, 6 months, 9 months and 1 year, answer each question again to see if you respond differently

1. When I give, it is more important that I give to..
    A. People in church because we have to look out for each other
    B. People at work so they can see I live the life I claim
    C. A homeless person when no one else is around
    D. People who give to me to show my appreciation

2. My intent is to love everyone but..
    A. I can only love close friends and family
    B. I only love people who have consistently shown me love
    C. I can't love people who have hurt me in the past
    D. No buts, I truly try to love everyone regardless of what they've done or who they are.

3. It is hard to find a church family or a home church because
    A. They don't understand me or my ways
    B. They want me to do things at church and I don't have time for that
    C. Once they find out what I have, they get jealous and don't want me around
    D. I have not been willing to change what I do or how I act

4. When determining what your gifts are, you should..
    A. Try everything until you find something you like, even if you're not that good at it.
    B. Pray constantly about it and willing to move if you are not in the right place
    C. Don't do anything but attend church until you're 100% sure
    D. Just do what your friends do so you'll enjoy it enough to stick with it.

5. I am not that good at praying, so I…
    A. Stopped trying because I don't know what I'm doing
    B. Only get prayer when I'm at church
    C. Just talk to God because I know he still hears me
    D. Rely on others to pray for me

Day 86

Mark 1 (New King James Version)

⁶ Now John was clothed with camel's hair and with a leather belt around his waist, and he ate locusts and wild honey. ⁷ And he preached, saying, "There comes One after me who is mightier than I, whose sandal strap I am not worthy to stoop down and loose. ⁸ I indeed baptized you with water, but He will baptize you with the Holy Spirit."

When you decided on your church and your pastor, what were you looking for? Did you choose the biggest church? Where you convinced that having a famous preacher would save you faster? Please understand this has nothing to do with the Pastor or the Church but your motives for your choice are the issue. Would you ever listen to anyone dressed as John was dressed?

Everyone poorly dressed is not guaranteed to be a false prophet nor is everyone impressively dressed guaranteed to be from God.

My thoughts about this scripture…

_____

_____

_____

_____

_____

Day 87

Mark 1 (New King James Version)

23 Now there was a man in their synagogue with an unclean spirit. And he cried out, 24 saying, "Let us alone! What have we to do with You, Jesus of Nazareth? Did You come to destroy us? I know who You are—the Holy One of God!"

25 But Jesus rebuked him, saying, "Be quiet, and come out of him!" 26 And when the unclean spirit had convulsed him and cried out with a loud voice, he came out of him. 27 Then they were all amazed, so that they questioned among themselves, saying, "What is this? What new doctrine is this? For with authority[f] He commands even the unclean spirits, and they obey Him." 28 And immediately His fame spread throughout all the region around Galilee.

Knowing that Jesus has the ability to remove anything unclean from your life, will you begin to call on him more?

_____
_____
_____
_____
_____

My thoughts about this scripture..

_____
_____
_____
_____
_____

Day 88

Deuteronomy 32 (New King James Version)

Give ear, O heavens, and I will speak;
And hear, O earth, the words of my mouth.
² Let my teaching drop as the rain,
My speech distill as the dew,
As raindrops on the tender herb,
And as showers on the grass.
³ For I proclaim the name of the LORD:
Ascribe greatness to our God.
⁴ He is the Rock, His work is perfect;
For all His ways are justice,
A God of truth and without injustice;
Righteous and upright is He.
⁵ "They have corrupted themselves;
They are not His children,
Because of their blemish:
A perverse and crooked generation.
⁶ Do you thus deal with the LORD,
O foolish and unwise people?
Is He not your Father, who bought you?
Has He not made you and established you?

Create 5 questions with answers from this scripture. Do not make them too easy so you will have to read to find the answers. This will help your studying and give you a better understanding of this scripture. **I'll do number "1" for you**.

1. The scripture describes Jesus' teachings as what?
   The raindrops on the tender herb and as the showers on the grass

2. _____

_____

_____

3. _____

_____

_____

4. _____

_____

_____

5. _____

_____

_____

Day 89

2 Timothy 3 (New King James Version)

*But know this, that in the last days perilous times will come: [2] For men will be lovers of themselves, lovers of money, boasters, proud, blasphemers, disobedient to parents, unthankful, unholy, [3] unloving, unforgiving, slanderers, without self-control, brutal, despisers of good, [4] traitors, headstrong, haughty, lovers of pleasure rather than lovers of God, [5] having a form of godliness but denying its power. And from such people turn away! [6] For of this sort are those who creep into households and make captives of gullible women loaded down with sins, led away by various lusts, [7] always learning and never able to come to the knowledge of the truth. [8] Now as Jannes and Jambres resisted Moses, so do these also resist the truth: men of corrupt minds, disapproved concerning the faith; [9] but they will progress no further, for their folly will be manifest to all, as theirs also wa*s.

"In the last days", this sounds a lot like how men are now. Don't continue to put off devoting your life to Christ because you may not have as much time as you think.

What I think about this scripture…

_____
_____
_____
_____
_____
_____
_____
_____

Day 90

Let's Review

Answer the following without searching for the answers to see how well you remember

1. The Bible consist of who many books? _____
2. The is the _____Testament and the _____Testament
3. Which testament is about Jesus' contributions on Earth? _____
4. How many disciples were with Jesus? _____
5. Which disciple was unfaithful to Jesus? _____
6. Name one prophet in the Bible. _____
7. Name a job of any disciple before following Jesus. _____
8. The Bible begins with the book of _____.
9. The last book of the Bible is _____.
10. One John was also known as John the _____.

Complete the following scriptures by memory. You can make correction if you need to later.

John 3 (New King James Version)

1. For God so loved the world

_____
_____

Deuteronomy 6:6-9 (New King James Version)

2. ^{6} "And these words which I

_____
_____
_____
_____
_____
_____
_____your gates.

Day 91

Deuteronomy 7 (New King James Version)

13 And He will love you and bless you and multiply you; He will also bless the fruit of your womb and the fruit of your land, your grain and your new wine and your oil, the increase of your cattle and the offspring of your flock, in the land of which He swore to your fathers to give you. 14 You shall be blessed above all peoples; there shall not be a male or female barren among you or among your livestock. 15 And the LORD will take away from you all sickness, and will afflict you with none of the terrible diseases of Egypt which you have known, but will lay them on all those who hate you. 16 Also you shall destroy all the peoples whom the LORD your God delivers over to you; your eye shall have no pity on them; nor shall you serve their gods, for that will be a snare to you.

My thoughts about this scripture

_____

_____

_____

_____

_____

_____

God has truly blessed me and…

_____

_____

_____

_____

_____

_____

Day 92

1. I know God has worked wonders in my life because..

    _____
    _____
    _____
    _____
    _____

2. In the past I would get really upset when _____ happened, now I just
    _____ because I realized _____
    _____.

3. My faith has grown greatly and I know that because.

    _____
    _____
    _____
    _____

4. Of all my changes, I am most pleased about _____

    _____
    _____
    _____
    _____

5. The one thing I really want to change is…

    _____
    _____
    _____
    _____
    _____

Day 93

2 Chronicles 31 (New King James Version)

And Azariah the chief priest, from the house of Zadok, answered him and said, "Since the people began to bring the offerings into the house of the LORD, we have had enough to eat and have plenty left, for the LORD has blessed His people; and what is left is this great abundance."

What I understand about tithing is..

_____
_____
_____
_____
_____

When I tithe I always…

_____
_____
_____

I don't tithe when..

_____
_____

Since I have began tithing consistently I..

_____
_____
_____
_____
_____

Day 94

Colossians 3 (New King James Version)

If then you were raised with Christ, seek those things which are above, where Christ is, sitting at the right hand of God. [2] Set your mind on things above, not on things on the earth. [3] For you died, and your life is hidden with Christ in God. [4] When Christ who is our life appears, then you also will appear with Him in glory.

[5] Therefore put to death your members which are on the earth: fornication, uncleanness, passion, evil desire, and covetousness, which is idolatry. [6] Because of these things the wrath of God is coming upon the sons of disobedience, [7] in which you yourselves once walked when you lived in them.

My thoughts about this scripture

_____
_____
_____
_____
_____

It is very difficult not to desire the things of this earth because..

_____
_____
_____
_____
_____

But knowing that, I try to..

_____
_____
_____
_____
_____

Day 95

Romans 12 (New King James Version)

I beseech you therefore, brethren, by the mercies of God, that you present your bodies a living sacrifice, holy, acceptable to God, which is your reasonable service. [2] And do not be conformed to this world, but be transformed by the renewing of your mind, that you may prove what is that good and acceptable and perfect will of God.

We would like to think that if we presented God with something it would be the best we had. Not the best of everything he may receive but the best of what we had to offer him. This scripture says to offer your body to God. This includes your mind, your heart and your soul. Would you feel comfortable giving God your mind knowing some of the thoughts you let hang around in there? I know we all manage to let some bad things slip in every once in a while but are you constantly thinking of bad things? Do some spring cleaning of your whole body and offer it to God. No, it doesn't have to be completely clean before giving it to Him but wouldn't you want to have made some efforts?

My thoughts about this scripture

_____
_____
_____
_____
_____
_____
_____
_____
_____
_____
_____

Spiritual Goals

```
R   A   R   F   K   L   H   D   F   S   Y   V   L   G   L
W   I   S   E   O   W   E   Q   G   P   N   L   L   O   U
H   K   G   V   V   S   H   D   M   I   I   O   O   C   F
D   K   E   H   S   I   E   W   A   R   R   L   L   H   E
N   D   A   E   T   Q   V   H   T   I   F   R   L   V   C
W   R   L   Y   T   E   V   E   F   T   Q   O   S   U   A
B   B   S   Q   M   Y   O   I   D   U   K   S   J   D   E
O   D   F   Q   N   C   E   U   V   A   M   H   O   D   P
T   S   E   T   K   D   G   R   S   L   W   O   Y   L   Y
M   R   U   T   Y   P   P   A   H   N   K   W   F   H   P
E   O   O   Y   F   P   R   A   I   S   E   D   U   X   H
X   X   N   F   F   I   X   V   N   O   H   S   L   W   F
O   H   X   Z   P   E   L   J   Q   Y   O   J   S   N   C
C   Y   G   Q   L   J   W   P   C   F   T   Z   G   N   T
D   E   M   E   E   D   E   R   U   I   L   Q   U   N   I
```

BLESSED	**GLORIFIED**	**HAPPY**
HOLY	**JOYFUL**	**LOVED**
PEACEFUL	**PRAISED**	**REDEEMED**
REVIVED	**RIGHTEOUSNESS**	**SPIRITUAL**
UPLIFTED		

Day 97

Malachi 3 (New King James Version)

[4] *"Then the offering of Judah and Jerusalem*
Will be pleasant to the LORD,
As in the days of old,
As in former years.
[5] *And I will come near you for judgment;*
I will be a swift witness
Against sorcerers,
Against adulterers,
Against perjurers,
Against those who exploit wage earners and widows and orphans,
And against those who turn away an alien—
Because they do not fear Me,"
Says the LORD of hosts.

My thoughts about this scripture

_____
_____
_____
_____
_____
_____

My biggest fear is being judged on

_____
_____
_____
_____
_____
_____

Day 98

The Book of Exodus

1. Exodus means
   A. To Excite and uplift
   B. To Exit
   C. To Exercise your rights
   D. To Exert

2. Moses fled to Midian because he….
   A. Needed to find a wife
   B. Killed an Egyptian
   C. Could not find work
   D. Found it was cooler weather there

3. Moses heard God's voice from
   A. The mouth of a sheep he was tending
   B. From a rain cloud as it passed
   C. A burning bush
   D. A fig tree

4. How many plagues did Pharaoh suffer
   A. 7
   B. 19
   C. 10
   D. 40

5. Why didn't Pharaoh fear the water plague
   A. Some magicians did the same thing
   B. The water began to clear up after a few minutes
   C. A worker for Pharaoh drank some of the water
   D. Pharaoh could also hear God's voice and knew his plan

6. The Most memorable part of Exodus is the
   A. Parting of the Red Sea
   B. Catching two boatloads of fish
   C. Jesus giving the blind man his sight
   D. Lot gathering his family and leaving his home

Day 99

Although Sonja lived in the city now with her husband, she is really a country girl. She was born in Georgia where she spent most of her childhood. Sonja worked for a brokerage firm and was very active in church. She also had a great husband who loved her dearly. In fact the only issue with Sonja is she didn't love herself. Sonja was above the average weight for someone her height. She tried diet after diet and gym memberships one after the other but nothing seemed to work. Fred, he husband, tried his best to convince her that his love for her wasn't based on her dress size. However, Sonja was determined to shed those unwanted pounds.

One evening Sonja was shopping for items to make her lunch for work. She was careful to check dietary content so she could effectively plan her meals each day. As she left the market and started to her car, she was approached by a young man. He stopped at the front of her car and began to talk to her.

"Good evening, my name is Luci. I know it sounds like a girl's name but what can you do?" Sonja laughed and spoke back to the gentleman. *"I'm sorry to bother you but I couldn't help noticing you purchased items that suggest you're watching your weight. Am I correct?"* "Yes", she replied. *"Well allow me to present you with the answer to all your issues".* He hands her a business card. *"Just visit the site and if you see something you like, you can purchase it online."* The man said. The card was white with the word **"LIVED"** in dark red letters across the front of it. She begins to read the card, *"LIVED, you haven't lived until you've lived life your way".* She looks up to ask a question and the man is gone. Sonja goes home, visits the site and purchases some of the items.

When the items she ordered arrives in the mail, the container looks just like the business card, white with big read letters **"LIVED"** across the front.   After a short period of time the product begins to work. She looses weight and everyone begins to notice, especially the men at her job. Sonja begins spending more time with her friends and at parties than she does with her husband. One night during a party at a co-workers' house she finds herself lip to lip with a man who is not her husband. Disappointed in herself and unwilling to keep it from him, she tells her husband what she had done. He explains that he knows he will have to forgive her one day but for now he has to leave. When she hears the door close behind him, she begins to cry uncontrollably. She notices the big white can that the diet powder came in. She picks up the can and begins yelling at it. *"This is all your fault, I've lost my husband, stopped going to church and embarrassed myself in front of my co-workers".*

Sonja slams the can down on the dresser and begins to cry again. As the can slides to a stop with the front of the can facing the mirror, the reflection shows the words on the can backwards. She looks at the can, now the big red letters read "**DEVIL**"

Day 100

After 100 days of learning more about the Bible, Studying God's word and establishing a more intimate relationship with Him. Let's see where you are.

Over the past few days I feel I have..

_____
_____
_____
_____
_____
_____
_____
_____
_____
_____
_____
_____

I still feel I need to..

_____
_____
_____
_____
_____
_____
_____
_____
_____
_____
_____
_____
_____
_____

Day 101

2 Corinthians 9 (New King James Version

⁶ But this I say: He who sows sparingly will also reap sparingly, and he who sows bountifully will also reap bountifully. ⁷ So let each one give as he purposes in his heart, not grudgingly or of necessity; for God loves a cheerful giver. ⁸ And God is able to make all grace abound toward you, that you, always having all sufficiency in all things, may have an abundance for every good work.

1. Do you feel that paying your tithes fulfills this request?
    _____
    _____

2. Are you convinced that money is the only thing you have to give?
    _____
    _____

3. If someone has money to pay their bills but no one to share their burdens are you there for them?
    _____
    _____

4. Sowing is what you give and reaping is what you get back. Which do you expect the most of sowing or reaping?
    _____
    _____

5. Is your giving from cheer or obligation?
    _____
    _____
    _____

Day 102

Complete the following;

Numbers 5:5-7 (New King James Version)

1. ⁵ Then the LORD spoke to Moses, saying, ⁶ "Speak to the children of Israel: 'When a man or woman

_____

⁷ then he shall confess

_____

_____

_____

2. Isaiah 59:1-3 (New King James Version)

Behold, the LORD's hand

_____

² But your iniquities

_____

³ For your hands

_____

_____

3. Micah 6:8 (New King James Version)

⁸ He has shown you,

_____

_____

_____

Day 103

2 Corinthians 1 (New King James Version)

[3] Blessed be the God and Father of our Lord Jesus Christ, the Father of mercies and God of all comfort, [4] who comforts us in all our tribulation, that we may be able to comfort those who are in any trouble, with the comfort with which we ourselves are comforted by God. [5] For as the sufferings of Christ abound in us, so our consolation also abounds through Christ. [6] Now if we are afflicted, it is for your consolation and salvation, which is effective for enduring the same sufferings which we also suffer. Or if we are comforted, it is for your consolation and salvation. [7] And our hope for you is steadfast, because we know that as you are partakers of the sufferings, so also you will partake of the consolation.

My thoughts about this scripture

_____
_____
_____
_____
_____
_____
_____
_____
_____
_____
_____
_____

In the future I will try to comfort others by..

_____
_____
_____
_____
_____
_____

Day 104

Knowing the Book

Across
2. ELIMELECH'S WIFE
3. RIGHTING A WRONG
5. BOOK 18 OF THE BIBLE
7. BIRTH PLACE OF JESUS
9. BETRAYED JESUS
Down
1. SAVIORS SHALL COME TO MOUNT ____
4. MANY FALSE ___ RISE UP AND DECEIVE
6. NUMBER OF MEN CHOSEN BY JESUS
8. PLACE OF ESCAPE FROM HEROD

Day 105

Luke 1 (New King James Version)

⁷⁰ As He spoke by the mouth of His holy prophets,
Who have been since the world began,
⁷¹ That we should be saved from our enemies
And from the hand of all who hate us,
⁷² To perform the mercy promised to our fathers
And to remember His holy covenant,
⁷³ The oath which He swore to our father Abraham:
⁷⁴ To grant us that we,
Being delivered from the hand of our enemies,
Might serve Him without fear,
⁷⁵ In holiness and righteousness before Him all the days of our life.

My thoughts about this scripture

_____
_____
_____
_____
_____
_____
_____
_____
_____
_____
_____
_____

Day 106

The Book of James 1

1. The number of Tribes
    A. 18
    B. 12
    C. 21
    D. 9

2. James 1:12 "Blessed is the man who endures ____"
    A. Power
    B. Sleepless days and nights
    C. Temptation
    D. His neighbors possessions

3. James 1:21 tells us to lay aside what?
    A. Lust and Greed
    B. Filthiness and Wickedness
    C. Money and Power
    D. Items for the future

4. A test of faith produces _____
    A. Patience
    B. Endurance
    C. Over confidence
    D. Sleepless Nights

5. Complete the following from James 1.

²² But be doers of the word,

_____

²³ For if anyone is a

_____

_____

Day 107

6 Now there was a day when the sons of God came to present themselves before the LORD, and Satan[b] also came among them. 7 And the LORD said to Satan, "From where do you come?"So Satan answered the LORD and said, "From going to and fro on the earth, and from walking back and forth on it."8 Then the LORD said to Satan, "Have you considered My servant Job, that there is none like him on the earth, a blameless and upright man, one who fears God and shuns evil?"

9 So Satan answered the LORD and said, "Does Job fear God for nothing? 10 Have You not made a hedge around him, around his household, and around all that he has on every side? You have blessed the work of his hands, and his possessions have increased in the land. 11 But now, stretch out Your hand and touch all that he has, and he will surely curse You to Your face!"

12 And the LORD said to Satan, "Behold, all that he has is in your power; only do not lay a hand on his person."

So Satan went out from the presence of the LORD. 13 Now there was a day when his sons and daughters were eating and drinking wine in their oldest brother's house; 14 and a messenger came to Job and said, "The oxen were plowing and the donkeys feeding beside them, 15 when the Sabeans[c] raided them and took them away—indeed they have killed the servants with the edge of the sword; and I alone have escaped to tell you!"

16 While he was still speaking, another also came and said, "The fire of God fell from heaven and burned up the sheep and the servants, and consumed them; and I alone have escaped to tell you!"

17 While he was still speaking, another also came and said, "The Chaldeans formed three bands, raided the camels and took them away, yes, and killed the servants with the edge of the sword; and I alone have escaped to tell you!"18 While he was still speaking, another also came and said, "Your sons and daughters were eating and drinking wine in their oldest brother's house, 19 and suddenly a great wind came from across[d] the wilderness and struck the four corners of the house, and it fell on the young people, and they are dead; and I alone have escaped to tell you!"20 Then Job arose, tore his robe, and shaved his head; and he fell to the ground and worshiped. 21 And he said:

*"Naked I came from my mother's womb,
And naked shall I return there.
The LORD gave, and the LORD has taken away;
Blessed be the name of the LORD."*

22 In all this Job did not sin nor charge God with wrong.

Still think you have the right to complain about your day?

Day 108

2 Timothy (New King James Version)

⁹ who has saved us and called us with a holy calling, not according to our works, but according to His own purpose and grace which was given to us in Christ Jesus before time began,

¹³ Hold fast the pattern of sound words which you have heard from me, in faith and love which are in Christ Jesus. ¹⁴ That good thing which was committed to you, keep by the Holy Spirit who dwells in us.

¹¹ This is a faithful saying:

For if we died with Him,
We shall also live with Him.
¹² If we endure,
We shall also reign with Him.
If we deny Him,
He also will deny us.
¹³ If we are faithless,
He remains faithful;
He cannot deny Himself.

How I feel about these scriptures

_____
_____
_____
_____
_____
_____

Being reassured in God's word means…

_____
_____
_____
_____
_____

Day 109

Wine is a mocker,
Strong drink is a brawler,
And whoever is led astray by it is not wise.

1. What is your understanding of this verse?

   _____
   _____
   _____
   _____

2. Do you feel that some people may use drinking as an excuse for bad behavior?

   _____
   _____
   _____
   _____

3. You are given a sound mind, how do you ensure you keep it?

   _____
   _____
   _____
   _____

Day 110

1 Peter 3 (New King James Version)

13 And who is he who will harm you if you become followers of what is good? 14 But even if you should suffer for righteousness' sake, you are blessed. "And do not be afraid of their threats, nor be troubled."[c] 15 But sanctify the Lord God[d] in your hearts, and always be ready to give a defense to everyone who asks you a reason for the hope that is in you, with meekness and fear; 16 having a good conscience, that when they defame you as evildoers, those who revile your good conduct in Christ may be ashamed. 17 For it is better, if it is the will of God, to suffer for doing good than for doing evil.

1. Are you more willing to please man than to please God?

   _____
   _____
   _____

2. What is your reason when people ask you why you follow Christ?

   _____
   _____
   _____

3. It is easier to do what is most popular, how do you prevent yourself from doing evil?

   _____
   _____
   _____

Number three asked about doing "Evil" not doing "Wrong". We all have our moments when we may stumble. The difference is "Wrong" is by accident "Evil" is with intention. So,

How do you prevent yourself from doing evil?

_____
_____
_____
_____

Day 111

Jeremiah 33 (New King James Version)

Moreover the word of the LORD came to Jeremiah a second time, while he was still shut up in the court of the prison, saying, [2] "Thus says the LORD who made it, the LORD who formed it to establish it (the LORD is His name): [3] 'Call to Me, and I will answer you, and show you great and mighty things, which you do not know.'

I believe we sometimes are under the misconception that God can only offer us what we see. We don't call to God because "we" don't see a way out of it or "we" don't see where the money can come from. God is not bound by our perception or understanding.

My thoughts about this scripture

_____
_____
_____
_____
_____
_____
_____

I always call on God because…

_____
_____
_____
_____
_____
_____
_____
_____
_____

Day 112

Review

1. Job 1 (New King James Version)

⁸ Then the LORD said to Satan, "Have you considered My servant ____ , that there is none like him on the earth, a blameless and upright man, one who fears God and shuns evil?"

    A. Lot
    B. Job
    C. Moses
    D. Jesus

2. Ezekiel 13 (New King James Version)

³ Thus says the Lord GOD: "Woe to the foolish _____ , who follow their own spirit and have seen nothing!

    A. Sinners
    B. Gentiles
    C. Prophets
    D. Pharaohs

3. Isaiah 59 (New King James Version)

² But your _____ have separated you from your God;

    A. Iniquities
    B. Country
    C. Family
    D. Choice of spouse

4. Boaz eventually married who?

    A. Ruth
    B. Mary
    C. Elizabeth
    D. Naomi

Day 113

Deuteronomy 32 (New King James Version)

16 They provoked Him to jealousy with foreign gods;
With abominations they provoked Him to anger.
17 They sacrificed to demons, not to God,
To gods they did not know,
To new gods, new arrivals
That your fathers did not fear.
18 Of the Rock who begot you, you are unmindful,
And have forgotten the God who fathered you.

I think in this case "foreign gods" could mean anything you envy, worship or put before God.

What I think about this scripture

_____
_____
_____
_____
_____

Do you *sometimes* forget who God is or what he has done for you?

If yes, explain when and what happened

_____
_____
_____
_____
_____
_____
_____

If no, explain how you prevent it from happening

_____
_____
_____
_____
_____
_____
_____

Day 114

Deuteronomy 5 (New King James Version)

*⁶ 'I am the L*ORD *your God who brought you out of the land of Egypt, out of the house of bondage.*

⁷ 'You shall have no other gods before Me.

*⁸ 'You shall not make for yourself a carved image—any likeness of anything that is in heaven above, or that is in the earth beneath, or that is in the water under the earth; ⁹ you shall not bow down to them nor serve them. For I, the L*ORD *your God, am a jealous God, visiting the iniquity of the fathers upon the children to the third and fourth generations of those who hate Me, ¹⁰ but showing mercy to thousands, to those who love Me and keep My commandments.*

*¹¹ 'You shall not take the name of the L*ORD *your God in vain, for the L*ORD *will not hold him guiltless who takes His name in vain.*

*¹² 'Observe the Sabbath day, to keep it holy, as the L*ORD *your God commanded you. ¹³ Six days you shall labor and do all your work, ¹⁴ but the seventh day is the Sabbath of the L*ORD *your God. In it you shall do no work: you, nor your son, nor your daughter, nor your male servant, nor your female servant, nor your ox, nor your donkey, nor any of your cattle, nor your stranger who is within your gates, that your male servant and your female servant may rest as well as you. ¹⁵ And remember that you were a slave in the land of Egypt, and the L*ORD *your God brought you out from there by a mighty hand and by an outstretched arm; therefore the L*ORD *your God commanded you to keep the Sabbath day.*

*¹⁶ 'Honor your father and your mother, as the L*ORD *your God has commanded you, that your days may be long, and that it may be well with you in the land which the L*ORD *your God is giving you.*

¹⁷ 'You shall not murder.

¹⁸ 'You shall not commit adultery.

¹⁹ 'You shall not steal.

²⁰ 'You shall not bear false witness against your neighbor.

²¹ 'You shall not covet your neighbor's wife; and you shall not desire your neighbor's house, his field, his male servant, his female servant, his ox, his donkey, or anything that is your neighbor's.

Day 115

Deuteronomy 6 (New King James Version)

[13] You shall fear the LORD your God and serve Him, and shall take oaths in His name. [14] You shall not go after other gods, the gods of the peoples who are all around you [15] (for the LORD your God is a jealous God among you), lest the anger of the LORD your God be aroused against you and destroy you from the face of the earth.

[16] "You shall not tempt the LORD your God as you tempted Him in Massah. [17] You shall diligently keep the commandments of the LORD your God, His testimonies, and His statutes which He has commanded you. [18] And you shall do what is right and good in the sight of the LORD, that it may be well with you, and that you may go in and possess the good land of which the LORD swore to your fathers, [19] to cast out all your enemies from before you, as the LORD has spoken.

1. Do you have a fear of God or do you feel you can pray your way out of anything?

    _____
    _____
    _____

2. What are some things you do that may be "Tempting God"?

    _____
    _____
    _____
    _____
    _____

3. Do you feel being obedient will help you possess the "good land" and still have your enemies casted out before you?

    _____
    _____
    _____
    _____
    _____

Day 116

Luke 8 (New King James Version)

38 Now the man from whom the demons had departed begged Him that he might be with Him. But Jesus sent him away, saying, 39 "Return to your own house, and tell what great things God has done for you." And he went his way and proclaimed throughout the whole city what great things Jesus had done for him.

What this scripture means to me

_____

_____

_____

_____

_____

_____

_____

_____

Why do you think Jesus required the man to return home instead of allowing him to follow?

_____

_____

_____

Day 117

Complete the following;

1. Zechariah 12 (New King James Version)

The burden[a] of the word of the LORD against Israel. Thus says the LORD,

_____
_____
_____

2. **Genesis 37 (New King James Version)**

³ Now Israel loved Joseph

_____
_____
_____.

⁴ But when his brothers saw

_____
_____
_____.

3. **1 Chronicles 13 (New King James Version)**

¹³ So David would not

_____
_____.

¹⁴ The ark of God remained

_____
_____
_____.

Day 118

The Book of Numbers

1. The Lord spoke to Moses in the wilderness of _____.
    A. Sinai
    B. The Red Sea
    C. Galilee
    D. Judea

2. When either a man or woman consecrates an offering to take the vow of Nazirite, to separate himself from the Lord. They also separate themselves from. (hint: numbers 6:?)
    A. Wine, grapes or anything produced by a grapevine
    B. Unleavened bread
    C. Partaking of meat from any fowl or bird
    D. Consuming swine or pig

3. Moses instructed Aaron to arrange seven _____. (numbers 8:?)
    A. Lambs
    B. Sheep
    C. Calves
    D. Lamps

4. Shelumiel was the son of _____. (numbers 10:?)
    A. Aaron
    B. Moses
    C. Zurishaddai
    D. Ahiezer

5. The Book of Numbers was the _____ Book of _____.
    A. 3RD of John
    B. 1ST of Moses
    C. 4TH of Moses
    D. 1ST of Paul

Day 119

This week I felt God tested me by

_____
_____
_____
_____
_____

I think I handled it like

_____
_____
_____
_____

I wish I handled it like

_____
_____
_____
_____

Here is the scripture I read to help me deal with it

_____
_____
_____
_____
_____
_____
_____
_____
_____
_____
_____

Day 120

Nehemiah 10 (New King James Version)

28 Now the rest of the people—the priests, the Levites, the gatekeepers, the singers, the Nethinim, and all those who had separated themselves from the peoples of the lands to the Law of God, their wives, their sons, and their daughters, everyone who had knowledge and understanding— 29 these joined with their brethren, their nobles, and entered into a curse and an oath to walk in God's Law, which was given by Moses the servant of God, and to observe and do all the commandments of the LORD our Lord, and His ordinances and His statutes

What I think about this scripture

_____
_____
_____
_____
_____
_____
_____
_____

Have you and your house agreed to walk in God's Law?

_____
_____

How do you during the day ensure you abide by that Law?

_____
_____
_____
_____

Do you check on the members of your family during the day to assist them with abiding in the Law?

_____
_____
_____
_____
_____

Day 121

The Book of Genesis

1. There was a river that ran out of Eden. That river became four riverheads, which were named? (Genesis 2:?)
   A. Pishon, Gihon, Hiddekel, Euphrates
   B. Pishon, Hiddekel, Posidon, Hippes
   C. Gihon, Hiddekel, Moses, Aaronous
   D. Pina, Nina, Santa Marie, Clara

2. Eve was formed by _____
   A. God using dust from the Garden of Eden
   B. God carving a woman from a tree stump and giving her life
   C. God taking a rib from Adam's side
   D. God creating Eve from a description provided by Adam

3. Eve was approached and questioned by what?
   A. A Serpent
   B. A Lamb
   C. A Bird
   D. A Lion

4. The name of the first two sons of Adam and Eve were?
   A. Salem and Ephram
   B. Cain and Abel
   C. Moses and Aaron
   D. David and Elijah

5. In the beginning God created the heavens and the earth, God said "Let there be"…
   A. Life
   B. Man
   C. Light
   D. Love

Day 122

The Old Testament

```
V A H U L J M H K C E D H H E
R M N A O E A U H L G E A A X
E O L S I I I R H E D U I I O
H S H A M N O K N A A T D R D
T U R E M N A E E U N E A A U
S Z H J I E S H K Z I R B H S
E E O C J I N G P Y E O O C H
N B L Y S E Y T N E L N M E A
S E G D U J R G A I Z O L Z B
S U C I T I V E L T K M A H A
P R O V E R B S M E I Y S T K
S R E B M U N X T I U O P U K
X L C M A L A C H I A M N R U
I S A I A H I A G G A H A S K
H O S E A H A N O J O E L S D
```

AMOS	CHRONICLES	DANIEL
DEUTERONOMY	ESTHER	EXODUS
EZEKIEL	EZRA	GENESIS
HABAKKUK	HAGGAI	HOSEA
ISAIAH	JEREMIAH	JOB
JOEL	JONAH	JOSHUS
JUDGES	KINGS	LAMENTATIONS
LEVITICUS	MALACHI	NAHUM
NEHEMIAH	NUMBERS	OBADIAH
PROVERBS	PSALM	RUTH
SAMUEL	ZECHARIAH	ZEPHANIAH

Day 123

Nahum 1 (New King James Version)

² God is jealous, and the LORD avenges;
The LORD avenges and is furious.
The LORD will take vengeance on His adversaries,
And He reserves wrath for His enemies;
³ The LORD is slow to anger and great in power,
And will not at all acquit the wicked.

My thoughts about this scripture

_____
_____
_____
_____
_____
_____
_____

Although the Bible says God is slow to anger I …

_____
_____
_____
_____
_____
_____
_____

Day 124

2 Peter 1 (New King James Version)

⁵ But also for this very reason, giving all diligence, add to your faith virtue, to virtue knowledge, ⁶ to knowledge self-control, to self-control perseverance, to perseverance godliness, ⁷ to godliness brotherly kindness, and to brotherly kindness love. ⁸ For if these things are yours and abound, you will be neither barren nor unfruitful in the knowledge of our Lord Jesus Christ. ⁹ For he who lacks these things is shortsighted, even to blindness, and has forgotten that he was cleansed from his old sins.

¹⁰ Therefore, brethren, be even more diligent to make your call and election sure, for if you do these things you will never stumble; ¹¹ for so an entrance will be supplied to you abundantly into the everlasting kingdom of our Lord and Savior Jesus Christ.

It is almost impossible to incorporate these things into your daily life if you are not conscience of what you are doing, what do you do daily to ensure you are fruitful?

_____
_____
_____
_____
_____
_____

If you are not being diligent to *"make your call"*, how can you begin to change that?

_____
_____
_____
_____
_____
_____
_____

Day 125

Isaiah 37 (New King James Version)

28 "But I know your dwelling place,
Your going out and your coming in,
And your rage against Me.
29 Because your rage against Me and your tumult
Have come up to My ears,
Therefore I will put My hook in your nose
And My bridle in your lips,
And I will turn you back
By the way which you came."'

My thoughts about this scripture

_____
_____
_____
_____
_____
_____
_____

Do you often blame God for things? If so how do you react towards him?

_____
_____
_____
_____
_____
_____
_____
_____
_____
_____
_____
_____
_____
_____
_____

Day 126

Job 42 (New King James Version)

⁷ And so it was, after the LORD had spoken these words to Job, that the LORD said to Eliphaz the Temanite, "My wrath is aroused against you and your two friends, for you have not spoken of Me what is right, as My servant Job has. ⁸ Now therefore, take for yourselves seven bulls and seven rams, go to My servant Job, and offer up for yourselves a burnt offering; and My servant Job shall pray for you. For I will accept him, lest I deal with you according to your folly; because you have not spoken of Me what is right, as My servant Job has."

My thoughts about this scripture

_____
_____
_____
_____
_____
_____
_____

Like Job was to these men, do you have someone who can help you? How?

_____
_____
_____
_____
_____
_____
_____

Psalm 127 (New King James Version)

Unless the LORD builds the house,
They labor in vain who build it;
Unless the LORD guards the city,
The watchman stays awake in vain.
[2] It is vain for you to rise up early,
To sit up late,
To eat the bread of sorrows;
For so He gives His beloved sleep.

My thoughts about this scripture

_____
_____
_____
_____
_____
_____

Has the Lord built your house?

_____
_____

What is meant by "in vain"?

_____
_____
_____
_____

Day 128

Luke 2 (New King James Version)

45 So when they did not find Him, they returned to Jerusalem, seeking Him. 46 Now so it was that after three days they found Him in the temple, sitting in the midst of the teachers, both listening to them and asking them questions. 47 And all who heard Him were astonished at His understanding and answers. 48 So when they saw Him, they were amazed; and His mother said to Him, "Son, why have You done this to us? Look, Your father and I have sought You anxiously."

49 And He said to them, "Why did you seek Me? Did you not know that I must be about My Father's business?" 50 But they did not understand the statement which He spoke to them.

Now Jesus was actually left behind but I want to use that to ask you a question.

1. If you were lost, would you find a church to ask directions?

_____
_____
_____

My thoughts about this scripture

_____
_____
_____
_____
_____
_____

Day 129

John 3 (New King James Version)

⁵ Jesus answered, "Most assuredly, I say to you, unless one is born of water and the Spirit, he cannot enter the kingdom of God. ⁶ That which is born of the flesh is flesh, and that which is born of the Spirit is spirit. ⁷ Do not marvel that I said to you, 'You must be born again.'

My thoughts about this scripture

_____

_____

_____

_____

_____

_____

Do you believe your spirit can be reborn if you mind remains in the flesh?

_____

_____

_____

_____

Do you feel you have to make up your mind that you are going to live for God first or can you just get saved and hope you eventually begin acting like it?

_____

_____

_____

_____

_____

Day 130

Revelation 11 (New King James Version)

^{17} saying:

"We give You thanks, O Lord God Almighty,
The One who is and who was and who is to come,[g]
Because You have taken Your great power and reigned.
^{18} The nations were angry, and Your wrath has come,
And the time of the dead, that they should be judged,
And that You should reward Your servants the prophets and the saints,
And those who fear Your name, small and great,
And should destroy those who destroy the earth."

My thoughts about this scripture

_____
_____
_____
_____
_____
_____

Do you fear God and his wrath?

_____

If yes, how will you avoid it?

_____
_____
_____

If no, how will you handle it?

_____
_____
_____

Day 131

Romans 8 (New King James Version)

²⁶ Likewise the Spirit also helps in our weaknesses. For we do not know what we should pray for as we ought, but the Spirit Himself makes intercession for us[b] with groanings which cannot be uttered. ²⁷ Now He who searches the hearts knows what the mind of the Spirit is, because He makes intercession for the saints according to the will of God.

The first eight words of this scripture express so much, we do have weaknesses and we do fall short sometimes. You do not have to pursue perfection as it is not obtainable for us nor is it required of us. Do the very best you can and rely on your help, lean on the Holy Spirit at all times.

1. When I fall short, I usually…..
     A. Fill bad the remainder of the day
     B. Ask God to forgive me and try to do better
     C. Complain about it to my friends and sometimes take it out on them too
     D. Think about giving up because I can't get this Christian thing right

2.   I understand now that the Holy Spirit…
_____
_____
_____
_____
_____
_____

Day 132

Complete the following;

1. 2 Chronicles 14 (New King James Version)

²Asa did what was good and _____ ,
³for he removed the _____
_____ .

2. Proverbs 30 (New King James Version)

⁴Who has _____ *?*
Who has _____ *?*
Who has _____ *?*
Who has _____ *?*
What is His _____ ,
If you know?

3. Obadiah 1 (New King James Version)

¹⁵ "For the day of the LORD _____
_____
_____
_____
_____

Proverbs 7 (New King James Version)

24 Now therefore, listen to me, my children;
Pay attention to the words of my mouth:
25 Do not let your heart turn aside to her ways,
Do not stray into her paths;
26 For she has cast down many wounded,
And all who were slain by her were strong men.
27 Her house is the way to hell,[b]
Descending to the chambers of death.

1. Why do you feel the word "Her" is used to describe this temptation?

   _____

   _____

2. How do you stay on your path?

   _____

   _____

   _____

   _____

3. What is your understanding of *"all who were slain by her were strong men"*?

   _____

   _____

   _____

   _____

   _____

   _____

Day 134

Write your favorite verse from the Bible

_____
_____
_____
_____
_____

Why is it your favorite?

_____
_____
_____
_____
_____

How it as changed or influenced my life

_____
_____
_____
_____
_____

Day 135

Romans 7 (New King James Version)

[5] For when we were in the flesh, the sinful passions which were aroused by the law were at work in our members to bear fruit to death. [6] But now we have been delivered from the law, having died to what we were held by, so that we should serve in the newness of the Spirit and not in the oldness of the letter.

My thoughts about this scripture

_____
_____
_____
_____
_____

The old me in the flesh

_____
_____
_____
_____

The new me in the newness of the Spirit

_____
_____
_____
_____
_____
_____
_____

Day 136

Romans 7 (New King James Version)

21 I find then a law, that evil is present with me, the one who wills to do good. 22 For I delight in the law of God according to the inward man. 23 But I see another law in my members, warring against the law of my mind, and bringing me into captivity to the law of sin which is in my members. 24 O wretched man that I am! Who will deliver me from this body of death? 25 I thank God—through Jesus Christ our Lord!

My thoughts about this scripture

_____
_____
_____
_____
_____
_____

My biggest struggles with my flesh and my mind are…

_____
_____
_____
_____
_____
_____
_____
_____

Knowing that God will deliver me from those issues is wonderful but I know I have to..

_____
_____
_____
_____
_____
_____
_____
_____

Day 137

James 4 (New King James Version)

Where do wars and fights come from among you? Do they not come from your desires for pleasure that war in your members? [2] You lust and do not have. You murder and covet and cannot obtain. You fight and war. Yet[a] you do not have because you do not ask. [3] You ask and do not receive, because you ask amiss, that you may spend it on your pleasures. [4] Adulterers and[b] adulteresses! Do you not know that friendship with the world is enmity with God? Whoever therefore wants to be a friend of the world makes himself an enemy of God. [5] Or do you think that the Scripture says in vain, "The Spirit who dwells in us yearns jealously"?

[6] But He gives more grace. Therefore He says:

"God resists the proud,
But gives grace to the humble."[c]

1. Do you believe that the "wars" are also in our homes? In our relationships? In our everyday struggles to walk in the Spirit?

   _____
   _____
   _____
   _____
   _____

2. When you ask of God are your prayers selfish?

   _____
   _____
   _____

3. We tend to lean more towards what we can see, hear, taste and feel which is why so many of us choose earthly desires over Heavenly treasures. What do you do to resist becoming a friend of the world?

   _____
   _____
   _____
   _____
   _____
   _____
   _____
   _____
   _____

Day 138

Philemon 1 (New King James Version)

⁴ I thank my God, making mention of you always in my prayers, ⁵ hearing of your love and faith which you have toward the Lord Jesus and toward all the saints, ⁶ that the sharing of your faith may become effective by the acknowledgment of every good thing which is in you[b] in Christ Jesus. ⁷ For we have[c] great joy[d] and consolation in your love, because the hearts of the saints have been refreshed by you, brother.

Could this letter be addressed to you?

_____

_____

Do you feel you represent Christ in a way that truly expresses the things you say?

_____

_____

My thoughts about this scripture

_____

_____

_____

_____

_____

_____

_____

Day 139

James 1 (New King James Version)

² My brethren, count it all joy when you fall into various trials, ³ knowing that the testing of your faith produces patience. ⁴ But let patience have its perfect work, that you may be perfect and complete, lacking nothing. ⁵ If any of you lacks wisdom, let him ask of God, who gives to all liberally and without reproach, and it will be given to him. ⁶ But let him ask in faith, with no doubting, for he who doubts is like a wave of the sea driven and tossed by the wind. ⁷ For let not that man suppose that he will receive anything from the Lord; ⁸ he is a double-minded man, unstable in all his ways.

My thoughts about this scripture

_____
_____
_____
_____
_____
_____
_____

My patience is..

_____
_____
_____
_____
_____

When I ask of God and I don't see change right away I..

_____
_____
_____
_____
_____
_____

Day 140

1 Timothy 1 (New King James Version)

³ As I urged you when I went into Macedonia—remain in Ephesus that you may charge some that they teach no other doctrine, ⁴ nor give heed to fables and endless genealogies, which cause disputes rather than godly edification which is in faith. ⁵ Now the purpose of the commandment is love from a pure heart, from a good conscience, and from sincere faith, ⁶ from which some, having strayed, have turned aside to idle talk, ⁷ desiring to be teachers of the law, understanding neither what they say nor the things which they affirm.

1. Are you more willing to tell someone you don't know the answer or are you willing to provide the wrong information about Christ to make you look better?

_____
_____
_____
_____

2. When you discuss the Bible, do you think it is important to only speak about things you understand yourself? Why or why not?

_____
_____
_____
_____
_____

3. Do you leave Bible study or Sunday school not understanding because you are too ashamed to ask questions? Why or why not?

_____
_____
_____
_____
_____
_____

Day 141

Locate and write the following;

1. Judges 3:1-2 (New King James Version)

_____
_____
_____
_____
_____
_____
_____

2. Proverbs 27:1 (New King James Version)

_____
_____
_____

3. 3 John 1:11 (New King James Version)

_____
_____
_____
_____

4. Exodus 8:22 (New King James Version)

_____
_____
_____
_____
_____

Day 142

Exodus 7 (New King James Version)

⁶ Then Moses and Aaron did so; just as the LORD commanded them, so they did. ⁷ And Moses was eighty years old and Aaron eighty-three years old when they spoke to Pharaoh.

At any age we can follow God's will. Please don't allow anyone to convince you that your age eliminates you from being saved. At eighty-three Moses and Aaron were leading thousands to God, surely at any age, you can lead yourself.

I sometimes think I've done wrong too long to be forgiven.

_____
_____
_____

I have allowed too much time to pass my plan now is to…

_____
_____
_____
_____
_____

I will continue to do God's will regardless of age and..

_____
_____
_____
_____

Day 143

Try to complete the following without your Bible. It doesn't matter if you can not remember them all or in the correct order, you will eventually.

Name the Books of the Old Testament;

1. _____
2. _____
3. _____
4. _____
5. _____
6. _____
7. _____
8. _____
9. _____
10. _____
11. _____
12. _____
13. _____
14. _____
15. _____
16. _____
17. _____
18. _____
19. _____
20. _____
21. _____
22. _____
23. _____
24. _____
25. _____
26. _____
27. _____
28. _____
29. _____
30. _____
31. _____
32. _____
33. _____
34. _____
35. _____

36. _____
37. _____
38. _____
39. _____

Day 144

Genesis 3 (New King James Version)

*Now the serpent was more cunning than any beast of the field which the L*ORD *God had made. And he said to the woman, "Has God indeed said, 'You shall not eat of every tree of the garden'?"*

² And the woman said to the serpent, "We may eat the fruit of the trees of the garden; ³ but of the fruit of the tree which is in the midst of the garden, God has said, 'You shall not eat it, nor shall you touch it, lest you die.'"

⁴ Then the serpent said to the woman, "You will not surely die. ⁵ For God knows that in the day you eat of it your eyes will be opened, and you will be like God, knowing good and evil."

My thoughts about this scripture

_____
_____
_____
_____
_____
_____
_____

I know God has no intentions of ever deceiving me so when he tells me something I....

_____
_____
_____
_____
_____
_____

The Bible gives us warnings that, like Eve, we will be approached by a serpent. However, he will be in the form of false prophets, those claiming to be Christ. The Bible even warns us that many of us will be fooled. How are you preparing yourself for the serpent?

Day 145

Mark 15 (New King James Version)

Immediately, in the morning, the chief priests held a consultation with the elders and scribes and the whole council; and they bound Jesus, led Him away, and delivered Him to Pilate. [2] Then Pilate asked Him, "Are You the King of the Jews?"

He answered and said to him, "It is as you say."

[3] And the chief priests accused Him of many things, but He answered nothing. [4] Then Pilate asked Him again, saying, "Do You answer nothing? See how many things they testify against You!"[a] [5] But Jesus still answered nothing, so that Pilate marveled.

My thoughts about this scripture

_____
_____
_____
_____
_____
_____

Jesus was tremendously confident in who he was and he knew God was with him Do you think we spend more time trying to prove to _people_ we are Christ's rather than just showing Christ that we believe we are His?

_____
_____
_____
_____
_____
_____

Day 146

Some thoughts for you today

A soft answer turns away wrath,
But a harsh word stirs up anger.
[2] The tongue of the wise uses knowledge rightly,
But the mouth of fools pours forth foolishness

[25] The LORD will destroy the house of the proud,
But He will establish the boundary of the widow.

[3] Commit your works to the LORD,
And your thoughts will be established.

[9] A man's heart plans his way,
But the LORD directs his steps

My thoughts about these verses

_____
_____
_____
_____
_____
_____
_____
_____
_____

Day 147

Ezra 8 (New King James Version)

²¹ Then I proclaimed a fast there at the river of Ahava, that we might humble ourselves before our God, to seek from Him the right way for us and our little ones and all our possessions. ²² For I was ashamed to request of the king an escort of soldiers and horsemen to help us against the enemy on the road, because we had spoken to the king, saying, "The hand of our God is upon all those for good who seek Him, but His power and His wrath are against all those who forsake Him." ²³ So we fasted and entreated our God for this, and He answered our prayer.

My thoughts about this scripture

_____
_____
_____
_____
_____
_____

What do you expect to accomplish when you fast?

_____
_____
_____
_____

Day 148

Matthew 19:24 (New King James Version)

24 And again I say to you, it is easier for a camel to go through the eye of a needle than for a rich man to enter the kingdom of God."

Do you allow money to prevent you from growing in Christ?

_____
_____
_____

Are you sure? Here is a way to check.

        A. Do you refuse to help people less fortunate?
        B. Have you ever lied or stolen to have more money?
        C. Do you choose making money over spending time with your family?
        D. Do you not pay your tithes because you think you are giving too much money to God?

Did you answer yes to any of these?

_____

Do you think the reason God has not blessed you with a lot of money is because you are not ready to handle it?

_____
_____

Even more, do you think God may be protecting you from missing Heaven because of how you may act if you had tons of money?

_____
_____

Just another reason to tell God, Thank you!!!

Day 149

Ecclesiastes 9 (New King James Version)

5 For the living know that they will die;
But the dead know nothing,
And they have no more reward,
For the memory of them is forgotten.
6 Also their love, their hatred, and their envy have now perished;
Nevermore will they have a share
In anything done under the sun.

7 Go, eat your bread with joy,
And drink your wine with a merry heart;
For God has already accepted your works.
8 Let your garments always be white,
And let your head lack no oil.

My thoughts about this scripture

_____
_____
_____
_____
_____
_____
_____

What do you think "Let your garments always be white" means?

_____
_____
_____
_____

Day 150

Ecclesiastes 4 (New King James Version)

4 Again, I saw that for all toil and every skillful work a man is envied by his neighbor. This also is vanity and grasping for the wind.

5 The fool folds his hands
And consumes his own flesh.
6 Better a handful with quietness
Than both hands full, together with toil and grasping for the wind.

About this scripture

_____
_____
_____
_____
_____
_____
_____
_____
_____

Day 151

Brandon was a machine operator in a factory that packaged meats. Brandon enjoyed his job, his co-workers and he had a very nice boss. Before beginning work there was always a meeting so Jeff, his boss, could explain what the shipments were and which had priority. During this meeting Jeff also explained that the company had acquired a new client who specialized in steaks. After work one evening, Brandon noticed another machine operator putting steaks into his back pack. After a few days, during another morning meeting, Jeff mentioned that some of the orders where short and the new client was accusing their company of taking the steaks. Jeff asked if everyone was doing everything to right way so he could go to the new client and defend his company and employers with a clear conscience.

Everyone expressed to Jeff that they were not stealing and it had to be a mistake in the amount they received. Everyone, including the employee Brandon saw taking the meat. Brandon was at a crossroad and had no idea which way to turn. Allowing Jeff to put the reputation of his company on the line could really hurt his business in the future. Besides, what if that caused him to lose his job.

Brandon waited to everyone had gone back to their machines and he went into the restroom. He used an old receipt in his wallet to write a note to Jeff explaining what he saw. He did not sign his name to it but he knew he couldn't stand by and do nothing.

A few days later, Brandon noticed the employee who he saw stealing was no longer there. He asked someone what happened and they explained he was the one stealing the steaks. Later that evening Jeff walked by Brandon and asked him if he could work a few hours over. Brandon said yes and Jeff thanked him. As he shock Brandon's hand he made eye contact and thanked him again. As they shock hands Brandon could feel Jeff putting something in his hand.

When Brandon had a chance and when no one was around, he pulled the paper from his pocket to see what Jeff had given him. It was the note he had left explaining what he saw. He didn't understand how Jeff knew it was him. After work he walked into the office and asked Jeff how he knew.

Jeff explained that there are cameras throughout the building and they knew he was taking them. He also explained that the camera recording him, seeing the guy steal the meat and they were not sure if the two of them were working together.

Brandon left work relieved that his honesty had saved his job.

Day 152

Joel 2 (New King James Version)

12 "Now, therefore," says the LORD,
"Turn to Me with all your heart,
With fasting, with weeping, and with mourning."
13 So rend your heart, and not your garments;
Return to the LORD your God,
For He is gracious and merciful,
Slow to anger, and of great kindness;
And He relents from doing harm

When I read this I think..

_____
_____
_____
_____
_____
_____

Have you given the Lord all your heart?

_____
_____

Knowing that the Lord is merciful and gracious do you find it easier to come to him for forgiveness or do you use that as a reason to continue being disobedient?

_____
_____
_____
_____
_____
_____
_____

Day 153

Genesis 3 (New King James Version)

¹² Then the man said, "The woman whom You gave to be with me, she gave me of the tree, and I ate."

Is there someone that you feel is preventing you from following God's will?
_____

There may be someone who suggest you do everything but follow God, everything but do good but the blame is still on you for listening to them.

I agree because..
_____
_____
_____
_____
_____

I disagree because…
_____
_____
_____
_____
_____

Day 154

Genesis 9 (New King James Version)

18 Now the sons of Noah who went out of the ark were Shem, Ham, and Japheth. And Ham was the father of Canaan. 19 These three were the sons of Noah, and from these the whole earth was populated.

So if the earth was populated by Noah's three sons, aren't we all related?

_____
_____
_____
_____
_____

My thoughts about this scripture

_____
_____
_____
_____
_____
_____
_____
_____
_____
_____

Day 155

Acts 4 (New King James Version)

⁵ And it came to pass, on the next day, that their rulers, elders, and scribes, ⁶ as well as Annas the high priest, Caiaphas, John, and Alexander, and as many as were of the family of the high priest, were gathered together at Jerusalem. ⁷ And when they had set them in the midst, they asked, "By what power or by what name have you done this?"

⁸ Then Peter, filled with the Holy Spirit, said to them, "Rulers of the people and elders of Israel: ⁹ If we this day are judged for a good deed done to a helpless man, by what means he has been made well, ¹⁰ let it be known to you all, and to all the people of Israel, that by the name of Jesus Christ of Nazareth, whom you crucified, whom God raised from the dead, by Him this man stands here before you whole. ¹¹ This is the 'stone which was rejected by you builders, which has become the chief cornerstone.'[a] ¹² Nor is there salvation in any other, for there is no other name under heaven given among men by which we must be saved."

My thoughts about this scripture

_____

_____

_____

_____

_____

What do you think is meant by the phrase "*This is the 'stone which was rejected by you builders, which has become the chief cornerstone*"?

_____

_____

_____

_____

_____

Day 156

Haggai 2 (New King James Version)

⁶ "For thus says the LORD of hosts: 'Once more (it is a little while) I will shake heaven and earth, the sea and dry land; ⁷ and I will shake all nations, and they shall come to the Desire of All Nations,[b] and I will fill this temple with glory,' says the LORD of hosts. ⁸ 'The silver is Mine, and the gold is Mine,' says the LORD of hosts. ⁹ 'The glory of this latter temple shall be greater than the former,' says the LORD of hosts. 'And in this place I will give peace,' says the LORD of hosts."

My thoughts about this scripture

_____
_____
_____
_____
_____
_____

"The silver is Mine, and the gold is Mine" , Why do you think the Lord said this?

_____
_____
_____
_____
_____
_____

Day 157

Genesis 32 (New King James Version)

22 And he arose that night and took his two wives, his two female servants, and his eleven sons, and crossed over the ford of Jabbok. 23 He took them, sent them over the brook, and sent over what he had. 24 Then Jacob was left alone; and a Man wrestled with him until the breaking of day. 25 Now when He saw that He did not prevail against him, He touched the socket of his hip; and the socket of Jacob's hip was out of joint as He wrestled with him. 26 And He said, "Let Me go, for the day breaks."

But he said, "I will not let You go unless You bless me!"

27 So He said to him, "What is your name?"

He said, "Jacob."

28 And He said, "Your name shall no longer be called Jacob, but Israel;[b] for you have struggled with God and with men, and have prevailed."

29 Then Jacob asked, saying, "Tell me Your name, I pray."

And He said, "Why is it that you ask about My name?" And He blessed him there.

My thoughts about this scripture

_____
_____
_____
_____
_____
_____
_____
_____
_____
_____
_____

Day 158

1 Samuel 9 (New King James Version)

There was a man of Benjamin whose name was Kish the son of Abiel, the son of Zeror, the son of Bechorath, the son of Aphiah, a Benjamite, a mighty man of power. ² *And he had a choice and handsome son whose name was Saul. There was not a more handsome person than he among the children of Israel. From his shoulders upward he was taller than any of the people.*

³ *Now the donkeys of Kish, Saul's father, were lost. And Kish said to his son Saul, "Please take one of the servants with you, and arise, go and look for the donkeys."* ⁴ *So he passed through the mountains of Ephraim and through the land of Shalisha, but they did not find them. Then they passed through the land of Shaalim, and they were not there. Then he passed through the land of the Benjamites, but they did not find them.*

1 Samuel 10 (New King James Version)

²¹ *And Saul answered and said, "Am I not a Benjamite, of the smallest of the tribes of Israel, and my family the least of all the families of the tribe* [a] *of Benjamin? Why then do you speak like this to me?"*

⁹ *So it was, when he had turned his back to go from Samuel, that God gave him another heart; and all those signs came to pass that day.* ¹⁰ *When they came there to the hill, there was a group of prophets to meet him; then the Spirit of God came upon him, and he prophesied among them.* ¹¹ *And it happened, when all who knew him formerly saw that he indeed prophesied among the prophets, that the people said to one another, "What is this that has come upon the son of Kish? Is Saul also among the prophets?"* ¹² *Then a man from there answered and said, "But who is their father?" Therefore it became a proverb: "Is Saul also among the prophets?"* ¹³ *And when he had finished prophesying, he went to the high place.*

My thoughts about how God uses least to achieve the most

_____
_____
_____
_____
_____
_____
_____

Day 159

James 5 (New King James Version)

Come now, you rich, weep and howl for your miseries that are coming upon you!
² Your riches are corrupted, and your garments are moth-eaten. ³ Your gold and silver are corroded, and their corrosion will be a witness against you and will eat your flesh like fire. You have heaped up treasure in the last days. ⁴ Indeed the wages of the laborers who mowed your fields, which you kept back by fraud, cry out; and the cries of the reapers have reached the ears of the Lord of Sabaoth.[a] ⁵ You have lived on the earth in pleasure and luxury; you have fattened your hearts as[b] in a day of slaughter.
⁶ You have condemned, you have murdered the just; he does not resist you.

My thoughts about this scripture

_____
_____
_____
_____
_____

Why do you think Bible suggest the wealthy may have trouble following God's word?

_____
_____
_____
_____
_____

If you pray for financial blessings, do you also pray for the wisdom you'll need as well?

_____
_____
_____
_____
_____

Day 160

Joshua 6 (New King James Version)

Now Jericho was securely shut up because of the children of Israel; none went out, and none came in. [2] And the LORD said to Joshua: "See! I have given Jericho into your hand, its king, and the mighty men of valor. [3] You shall march around the city, all you men of war; you shall go all around the city once. This you shall do six days. [4] And seven priests shall bear seven trumpets of rams' horns before the ark. But the seventh day you shall march around the city seven times, and the priests shall blow the trumpets. [5] It shall come to pass, when they make a long blast with the ram's horn, and when you hear the sound of the trumpet, that all the people shall shout with a great shout; then the wall of the city will fall down flat. And the people shall go up every man straight before him

My thoughts about this scripture

_____
_____
_____
_____
_____

Many may look at this as extreme but the focus should be on following God's directions.

I agree because

_____
_____
_____
_____

I disagree because

_____
_____
_____
_____

Day 161

Romans 10 (New King James Version)

5 For Moses writes about the righteousness which is of the law, "The man who does those things shall live by them."[b] 6 But the righteousness of faith speaks in this way, "Do not say in your heart, 'Who will ascend into heaven?'"[c] (that is, to bring Christ down from above) 7 or, "'Who will descend into the abyss?'"[d] (that is, to bring Christ up from the dead). 8 But what does it say? "The word is near you, in your mouth and in your heart"[e] (that is, the word of faith which we preach): 9 that if you confess with your mouth the Lord Jesus and believe in your heart that God has raised Him from the dead, you will be saved. 10 For with the heart one believes unto righteousness, and with the mouth confession is made unto salvation. 11 For the Scripture says, "Whoever believes on Him will not be put to shame."[f] 12 For there is no distinction between Jew and Greek, for the same Lord over all is rich to all who call upon Him. 13 For "whoever calls on the name of the LORD shall be saved."[g]

My thoughts about this scripture
_____
_____
_____
_____
_____
_____
_____
_____

Have you called on the name of the LORD to be saved?
_____

I truly believe in my heart that….
_____
_____
_____

Please contact your pastor and inquire more about confessing and being saved. And yes, your life does depend on it.

Psalm 105 (New King James Version)

*Oh, give thanks to the L*ORD*!*
Call upon His name;
Make known His deeds among the peoples!
[2] Sing to Him, sing psalms to Him;
Talk of all His wondrous works!
[3] Glory in His holy name;
*Let the hearts of those rejoice who seek the L*ORD*!*

Psalm 106 (New King James Version)

*[4] Remember me, O L*ORD*, with the favor You have toward Your people.*
Oh, visit me with Your salvation,
[5] That I may see the benefit of Your chosen ones,
That I may rejoice in the gladness of Your nation,
That I may glory with Your inheritance.

Psalm 7 (New King James Version)

*[17] I will praise the L*ORD *according to His righteousness,*
*And will sing praise to the name of the L*ORD *Most High.*

Psalm 10 (New King James Version)

*[16] The L*ORD *is King forever and ever;*
The nations have perished out of His land.
*[17] L*ORD*, You have heard the desire of the humble;*
You will prepare their heart;
You will cause Your ear to hear,
[18] To do justice to the fatherless and the oppressed,
That the man of the earth may oppress no more.

Day 163

Acts 19 (New King James Version)

And it happened, while Apollos was at Corinth, that Paul, having passed through the upper regions, came to Ephesus. And finding some disciples [2] he said to them, "Did you receive the Holy Spirit when you believed?"

So they said to him, "We have not so much as heard whether there is a Holy Spirit."

[3] And he said to them, "Into what then were you baptized?"

So they said, "Into John's baptism."

[4] Then Paul said, "John indeed baptized with a baptism of repentance, saying to the people that they should believe on Him who would come after him, that is, on Christ Jesus."

[5] When they heard this, they were baptized in the name of the Lord Jesus. [6] And when Paul had laid hands on them, the Holy Spirit came upon them, and they spoke with tongues and prophesied. [7] Now the men were about twelve in all.

[8] And he went into the synagogue and spoke boldly for three months, reasoning and persuading concerning the things of the kingdom of God. [9] But when some were hardened and did not believe, but spoke evil of the Way before the multitude, he departed from them and withdrew the disciples, reasoning daily in the school of Tyrannus. [10] And this continued for two years, so that all who dwelt in Asia heard the word of the Lord Jesus, both Jews and Greeks.

My thoughts about this scripture

_____
_____
_____
_____
_____
_____
_____
_____
_____

Day 164

Psalm 1 (New King James Version)

1 Blessed is the man
Who walks not in the counsel of the ungodly,
Nor stands in the path of sinners,
Nor sits in the seat of the scornful;
² But his delight is in the law of the LORD,
And in His law he meditates day and night.
³ He shall be like a tree
Planted by the rivers of water,
That brings forth its fruit in its season,
Whose leaf also shall not wither;
And whatever he does shall prosper.

⁴ The ungodly are not so,
But are like the chaff which the wind drives away.
⁵ Therefore the ungodly shall not stand in the judgment,
Nor sinners in the congregation of the righteous.

⁶ For the LORD knows the way of the righteous,
But the way of the ungodly shall perish.

My thoughts about this scripture

_____
_____
_____
_____
_____
_____
_____

Day 165

The Book of Job

1. Job was from the land of _____.
   A. Uz
   B. Oz
   C. Galilee
   D. Judea

2. Job was attacked by_____.
   A. Barbarians
   B. Romans
   C. Satan
   D. Moses

3. Job lost his _____ and _____.
   A. Silver and Gold
   B. Property and Children
   C. Donkeys and Sheep
   D. House and Wife

4. Satan accused God of having a _____ around Job
   A. Hedge
   B. Net
   C. Fence
   D. Guards

5. Job lost so much that he _____.
   A. Cursed God's name
   B. Fell to the ground and worshiped
   C. Took the few things he had left and moved
   D. Blamed his children and never talked to them again

Day 166

Job 1 (New King James Version)

⁶ Now there was a day when the sons of God came to present themselves before the LORD, and Satan[b] also came among them. ⁷ And the LORD said to Satan, "From where do you come?"

So Satan answered the LORD and said, "From going to and fro on the earth, and from walking back and forth on it."

⁸ Then the LORD said to Satan, "Have you considered My servant Job, that there is none like him on the earth, a blameless and upright man, one who fears God and shuns evil?"

⁹ So Satan answered the LORD and said, "Does Job fear God for nothing? ¹⁰ Have You not made a hedge around him, around his household, and around all that he has on every side? You have blessed the work of his hands, and his possessions have increased in the land. ¹¹ But now, stretch out Your hand and touch all that he has, and he will surely curse You to Your face!"

¹² And the LORD said to Satan, "Behold, all that he has is in your power; only do not lay a hand on his person."

My thoughts about this scripture

_____
_____
_____
_____
_____
_____
_____

Do you think that God allows Satan to tempt us because He knows with Him we have the power to resist?

_____
_____
_____
_____

Day 167

2 Samuel 22 (New King James Version)

Then David spoke to the LORD the words of this song, on the day when the LORD had delivered him from the hand of all his enemies, and from the hand of Saul. ² And he said:[a]

"The LORD is my rock and my fortress and my deliverer;
³ The God of my strength, in whom I will trust;
My shield and the horn of my salvation,
My stronghold and my refuge;
My Savior, You save me from violence.
⁴ I will call upon the LORD, who is worthy to be praised;
So shall I be saved from my enemies.

My thoughts about this scripture

_____
_____
_____
_____
_____
_____

Do you feel God is your everything?

_____
_____

Do you only feel that way right after He has done something for you?

_____
_____

What will convince you that he can provide whatever you need?

_____
_____
_____

Ways of Worship

```
G  J  C  B  F  F  S  S  P  N  Q  N  M  L  G
N  N  M  E  M  U  I  H  O  E  L  W  I  M  N
I  Z  I  Q  S  N  G  I  O  V  J  F  J  B  I
H  N  R  C  G  T  N  N  L  U  T  G  Y  O  H
C  D  W  I  I  U  E  B  I  I  T  J  I  O  T
A  Q  N  S  M  O  G  L  N  K  G  I  Y  Y  I
E  G  H  M  D  N  J  G  G  E  L  I  N  D  T
R  A  O  W  I  Q  H  E  L  R  M  A  G  G  D
P  C  G  V  S  A  K  X  R  P  B  O  T  A  A
N  P  R  C  N  O  I  T  A  T  I  D  E  M  N
X  E  M  D  C  L  A  P  P  I  N  G  C  S  C
S  E  S  G  N  I  Y  A  R  P  Y  E  H  L  I
H  E  A  L  I  N  G  J  P  E  H  F  B  I  N
P  J  T  U  S  X  S  M  K  W  W  F  T  J  G
W  Z  I  C  S  O  O  W  Z  Z  Q  Q  C  Y  H
```

CLAPPING	COMMUNION	DANCING
HEALING	LIFTINGHANDS	MEDITATION
PRAYING	PREACHING	REJOICING
SERVING	SHOUTING	SINGING
TALKING	TITHING	

Day 169

A Little inspiration for your day, enjoy yourself as you rejoice in the Lord

Philippians 4:4

Rejoice in the Lord always. I will say it again: Rejoice!

Psalm 13:5

But I trust in your unfailing love; my heart rejoices in your salvation.

1 Thessalonians 5:16-18

Be joyful always; pray continually; give thanks in all circumstances, for this is God's will for you in Christ Jesus.

Psalm 40:16

But may all who seek you rejoice and be glad in you; may those who love your salvation always say, "The LORD be exalted!"

James 1:2-4

Consider it pure joy, my brothers, whenever you face trials of many kinds, because you know that the testing of your faith develops perseverance. Perseverance must finish its work so that you may be mature and complete, not lacking anything.

Psalm 30:5

For his anger lasts only a moment, but his favor lasts a lifetime; weeping may remain for a night, but rejoicing comes in the morning.

Romans 5:1-4

Therefore, since we have been justified through faith, we have peace with God through our Lord Jesus Christ, through whom we have gained access by faith into this grace in which we now stand. And we rejoice in the hope of the glory of God. Not only so, but we also rejoice in our sufferings, because we know that suffering produces perseverance; perseverance, character; and character, hope.

Day 170

Psalm 37 (New King James Version)

7 Rest in the LORD, and wait patiently for Him;
Do not fret because of him who prospers in his way,
Because of the man who brings wicked schemes to pass.
8 Cease from anger, and forsake wrath;
Do not fret—it only causes harm.

My thoughts about these verses

_____
_____
_____

Do not fret because of evildoers,
Nor be envious of the workers of iniquity.
2 For they shall soon be cut down like the grass,
And wither as the green herb.

3 Trust in the LORD, and do good;
Dwell in the land, and feed on His faithfulness.
4 Delight yourself also in the LORD,
And He shall give you the desires of your heart.

My thoughts about these verses

_____
_____
_____

18 The LORD knows the days of the upright,
And their inheritance shall be forever.
19 They shall not be ashamed in the evil time,
And in the days of famine they shall be satisfied.
20 But the wicked shall perish;
And the enemies of the LORD,
Like the splendor of the meadows, shall vanish.
Into smoke they shall vanish away.

My thoughts about these verses

_____
_____
_____

Day 171

Philippians 4 (New King James Version)

⁵ Let your gentleness be known to all men. The Lord is at hand.

⁶ Be anxious for nothing, but in everything by prayer and supplication, with thanksgiving, let your requests be made known to God; ⁷ and the peace of God, which surpasses all understanding, will guard your hearts and minds through Christ Jesus

⁸ Finally, brethren, whatever things are true, whatever things are noble, whatever things are just, whatever things are pure, whatever things are lovely, whatever things are of good report, if there is any virtue and if there is anything praiseworthy— meditate on these things. ⁹ The things which you learned and received and heard and saw in me, these do, and the God of peace will be with you.

My thoughts about this scripture

_____
_____
_____
_____
_____
_____
_____
_____
_____

What do you think is meant by "*and the peace of God, which surpasses all understanding, will guard your hearts and minds through Christ Jesus*"?

_____
_____
_____
_____
_____

Day 172

Joel 2 (New King James Version)

Blow the trumpet in Zion,
And sound an alarm in My holy mountain!
Let all the inhabitants of the land tremble;
For the day of the LORD is coming,
For it is at hand:
² A day of darkness and gloominess,
A day of clouds and thick darkness,
Like the morning clouds spread over the mountains.
A people come, great and strong,
The like of whom has never been;
Nor will there ever be any such after them,
Even for many successive generations.

My thoughts about this scripture

_____
_____
_____
_____
_____

Are you constantly preparing for the day of the Lord?

_____
_____
_____

Day 173

Judges 3 (New King James Version)

⁷ So the children of Israel did evil in the sight of the LORD. They forgot the LORD their God, and served the Baals and Asherahs.[a] ⁸ Therefore the anger of the LORD was hot against Israel, and He sold them into the hand of Cushan-Rishathaim king of Mesopotamia; and the children of Israel served Cushan-Rishathaim eight years. ⁹ When the children of Israel cried out to the LORD, the LORD raised up a deliverer for the children of Israel, who delivered them: Othniel the son of Kenaz, Caleb's younger brother. ¹⁰ The Spirit of the LORD came upon him, and he judged Israel. He went out to war, and the LORD delivered Cushan-Rishathaim king of Mesopotamia into his hand; and his hand prevailed over Cushan-Rishathaim. ¹¹ So the land had rest for forty years. Then Othniel the son of Kenaz died

My thoughts about this scripture

_____
_____
_____
_____

Do you believe God punishes us when we do evil or do you believe he just doesn't protect us against it because we were disobedient?

_____
_____
_____
_____
_____

Although the children of Israel did evil they cried out to the Lord and he forgave them. So even when you do wrong do you understand you can still cry out to the Lord?

_____
_____
_____
_____

Day 174

Exodus 21 (New King James Version)

15 "And he who strikes his father or his mother shall surely be put to death.

My thoughts about this verse

_____

_____

_____

Exodus 22 (New King James Version)

20 "He who sacrifices to any god, except to the LORD only, he shall be utterly destroyed.

My thoughts about this verse

_____

_____

_____

28 "You shall not revile God, nor curse a ruler of your people.

My thoughts about this verse

_____

_____

_____

Exodus 23 (New King James Version)

You shall not circulate a false report. Do not put your hand with the wicked to be an unrighteous witness. 2 You shall not follow a crowd to do evil; nor shall you testify in a dispute so as to turn aside after many to pervert justice. 3 You shall not show partiality to a poor man in his dispute.

My thoughts about these verses

_____

_____

_____

_____

_____

Day 175

Colossians 3 (New King James Version)

⁸ But now you yourselves are to put off all these: anger, wrath, malice, blasphemy, filthy language out of your mouth. ⁹ Do not lie to one another, since you have put off the old man with his deeds, ¹⁰ and have put on the new man who is renewed in knowledge according to the image of Him who created him, ¹¹ where there is neither Greek nor Jew, circumcised nor uncircumcised, barbarian, Scythian, slave nor free, but Christ is all and in all.

Character of the New Man

¹² Therefore, as the elect of God, holy and beloved, put on tender mercies, kindness, humility, meekness, longsuffering; ¹³ bearing with one another, and forgiving one another, if anyone has a complaint against another; even as Christ forgave you, so you also must do. ¹⁴ But above all these things put on love, which is the bond of perfection. ¹⁵ And let the peace of God rule in your hearts, to which also you were called in one body; and be thankful. ¹⁶ Let the word of Christ dwell in you richly in all wisdom, teaching and admonishing one another in psalms and hymns and spiritual songs, singing with grace in your hearts to the Lord. ¹⁷ And whatever you do in word or deed, do all in the name of the Lord Jesus, giving thanks to God the Father through Him.

How have you changed from the "old man" to the "new man" in Christ?

_____
_____
_____
_____
_____
_____
_____

When I read this I think..

_____
_____
_____
_____
_____
_____
_____

Day 176

Deuteronomy 28 (New King James Version)

"Now it shall come to pass, if you diligently obey the voice of the LORD your God, to observe carefully all His commandments which I command you today, that the LORD your God will set you high above all nations of the earth. ² And all these blessings shall come upon you and overtake you, because you obey the voice of the LORD your God:

³ "Blessed shall you be in the city, and blessed shall you be in the country.

⁴ "Blessed shall be the fruit of your body, the produce of your ground and the increase of your herds, the increase of your cattle and the offspring of your flocks.

⁵ "Blessed shall be your basket and your kneading bowl.

⁶ "Blessed shall you be when you come in, and blessed shall you be when you go out.

⁷ "The LORD will cause your enemies who rise against you to be defeated before your face; they shall come out against you one way and flee before you seven ways.

⁸ "The LORD will command the blessing on you in your storehouses and in all to which you set your hand, and He will bless you in the land which the LORD your God is giving you.

⁹ "The LORD will establish you as a holy people to Himself, just as He has sworn to you, if you keep the commandments of the LORD your God and walk in His ways. ¹⁰ Then all peoples of the earth shall see that you are called by the name of the LORD, and they shall be afraid of you. ¹¹ And the LORD will grant you plenty of goods, in the fruit of your body, in the increase of your livestock, and in the produce of your ground, in the land of which the LORD swore to your fathers to give you. ¹² The LORD will open to you His good treasure, the heavens, to give the rain to your land in its season, and to bless all the work of your hand. You shall lend to many nations, but you shall not borrow. ¹³ And the LORD will make you the head and not the tail; you shall be above only, and not be beneath, if you heed the commandments of the LORD your God, which I command you today, and are careful to observe them. ¹⁴ So you shall not turn aside from any of the words which I command you this day, to the right or the left, to go after other gods to serve them.

My thoughts about this scripture

_____

_____

_____

_____

Day 177

Deuteronomy 30 (New King James Version)

Now it shall come to pass, when all these things come upon you, the blessing and the curse which I have set before you, and you call them to mind among all the nations where the LORD your God drives you, ² and you return to the LORD your God and obey His voice, according to all that I command you today, you and your children, with all your heart and with all your soul, ³ that the LORD your God will bring you back from captivity, and have compassion on you, and gather you again from all the nations where the LORD your God has scattered you. ⁴ If any of you are driven out to the farthest parts under heaven, from there the LORD your God will gather you, and from there He will bring you. ⁵ Then the LORD your God will bring you to the land which your fathers possessed, and you shall possess it. He will prosper you and multiply you more than your fathers. ⁶ And the LORD your God will circumcise your heart and the heart of your descendants, to love the LORD your God with all your heart and with all your soul, that you may live.

My thoughts about this scripture

_____
_____
_____
_____
_____
_____
_____

"If any of you are driven out to the farthest parts under heaven". Do you think this only means your physical location or does it also include where you are in your beliefs in Christ?

_____
_____
_____
_____
_____
_____
_____

Day 178

Jeremiah 20 (New King James Version)

¹¹ But the L<small>ORD</small> is with me as a mighty, awesome One.
Therefore my persecutors will stumble, and will not prevail.
They will be greatly ashamed, for they will not prosper.
Their everlasting confusion will never be forgotten.
¹² But, O L<small>ORD</small> of hosts,
You who test the righteous,
And see the mind and heart,
Let me see Your vengeance on them;
For I have pleaded my cause before You.

My thoughts about this scripture

_____
_____
_____
_____
_____
_____

Do you still waste time trying to fight against your enemies, even when God has promised He will take care of them?

_____
_____
_____
_____
_____
_____
_____

Day 179

Jeremiah 22 (New King James Version)

13 "Woe to him who builds his house by unrighteousness
And his chambers by injustice,
Who uses his neighbor's service without wages
And gives him nothing for his work,
14 Who says, 'I will build myself a wide house with spacious chambers,
And cut out windows for it,
Paneling it with cedar
And painting it with vermilion.'

My thoughts about this scripture

_____
_____
_____
_____
_____
_____
_____
_____

What do you build your house on?

_____
_____
_____
_____
_____
_____
_____

Day 180

Answer the following questions truthfully. Come back from time to time and see if your answers have changed.

How do you handle people that you don't particularly care for?

_____
_____
_____

How do you handle people you know don't particularly care for you?

_____
_____
_____

Have you ever addressed the issue as to why you feel the way you do about people?

_____
_____
_____

Are you more likely to speak to someone first or do you way to be spoken to?

_____
_____
_____

Do you find it difficult to forgive people? Why?

_____
_____
_____

Are you more likely to voice when you are displeased with someone or do you keep it to yourself? Explain.

_____
_____
_____
_____
_____

Day 181

Colossians 4 (New King James Version)

2 Continue earnestly in prayer, being vigilant in it with thanksgiving; 3 meanwhile praying also for us, that God would open to us a door for the word, to speak the mystery of Christ, for which I am also in chains, 4 that I may make it manifest, as I ought to speak.

5 Walk in wisdom toward those who are outside, redeeming the time. 6 Let your speech always be with grace, seasoned with salt, that you may know how you ought to answer each one.

My thoughts about this scripture

_____
_____
_____
_____
_____

What do you think "seasoned with salt" means?

_____
_____
_____

Day 182

1 Chronicles 10 (New King James Version)

13 So Saul died for his unfaithfulness which he had committed against the LORD, because he did not keep the word of the LORD, and also because he consulted a medium for guidance. 14 But he did not inquire of the LORD; therefore He killed him, and turned the kingdom over to David the son of Jesse.

My thoughts about this scripture

_____
_____
_____
_____
_____
_____

Are you obedient to God when you hear what you want but turn to other sources when your request us unanswered?

_____
_____
_____
_____
_____
_____

Do you think Saul's death for unfaithfulness can be compared to the death of our hopes and dreams if we are unfaithful?

_____
_____
_____
_____
_____
_____
_____

Day 183

Leviticus 19 (New King James Version)

⁹ 'When you reap the harvest of your land, you shall not wholly reap the corners of your field, nor shall you gather the gleanings of your harvest. ¹⁰ And you shall not glean your vineyard, nor shall you gather every grape of your vineyard; you shall leave them for the poor and the stranger: I am the LORD your God.

¹¹ 'You shall not steal, nor deal falsely, nor lie to one another. ¹² And you shall not swear by My name falsely, nor shall you profane the name of your God: I am the LORD.

¹³ 'You shall not cheat your neighbor, nor rob him. The wages of him who is hired shall not remain with you all night until morning. ¹⁴ You shall not curse the deaf, nor put a stumbling block before the blind, but shall fear your God: I am the LORD.

¹⁵ 'You shall do no injustice in judgment. You shall not be partial to the poor, nor honor the person of the mighty. In righteousness you shall judge your neighbor. ¹⁶ You shall not go about as a talebearer among your people; nor shall you take a stand against the life of your neighbor: I am the LORD.

¹⁷ 'You shall not hate your brother in your heart. You shall surely rebuke your neighbor, and not bear sin because of him. ¹⁸ You shall not take vengeance, nor bear any grudge against the children of your people, but you shall love your neighbor as yourself: I am the LORD.

¹⁹ 'You shall keep My statutes. You shall not let your livestock breed with another kind. You shall not sow your field with mixed seed. Nor shall a garment of mixed linen and wool come upon you.

My thoughts about these verses

_____
_____
_____
_____
_____
_____

After reading these, what do you feel you need to change?

_____
_____
_____

Day 184

Genesis 39 (New King James Version)

Now Joseph had been taken down to Egypt. And Potiphar, an officer of Pharaoh, captain of the guard, an Egyptian, bought him from the Ishmaelites who had taken him down there. [2] The LORD was with Joseph, and he was a successful man; and he was in the house of his master the Egyptian. [3] And his master saw that the LORD was with him and that the LORD made all he did to prosper in his hand. [4] So Joseph found favor in his sight, and served him. Then he made him overseer of his house, and all that he had he put under his authority. [5] So it was, from the time that he had made him overseer of his house and all that he had, that the LORD blessed the Egyptian's house for Joseph's sake; and the blessing of the LORD was on all that he had in the house and in the field. [6] Thus he left all that he had in Joseph's hand, and he did not know what he had except for the bread which he ate.

My thoughts about this scripture

_____
_____
_____
_____
_____

Even if you don't like your career choice, do you perform your job as a Christian to allow God to bless you and those around you?

_____
_____
_____

If you ask God for a better job but don't do you best in the one you have, do you feel you deserve another job?

_____
_____

As you are given more authority in your position is your focus giving God the glory and helping others or is it getting more for yourself? (be honest)

_____
_____
_____

Day 185

Proverbs 29 (New King James Version)

He who is often rebuked, *and* hardens *his* neck,
Will suddenly be destroyed, and that without remedy.

² When the righteous are in authority, the people rejoice;
But when a wicked *man* rules, the people groan.

³ Whoever loves wisdom makes his father rejoice,
But a companion of harlots wastes *his* wealth.

⁴ The king establishes the land by justice,
But he who receives bribes overthrows it.

⁵ A man who flatters his neighbor
Spreads a net for his feet.

⁶ By transgression an evil man is snared,
But the righteous sings and rejoices.

⁷ The righteous considers the cause of the poor,
But the wicked does not understand *such* knowledge.

⁸ Scoffers set a city aflame,
But wise *men* turn away wrath.

⁹ *If* a wise man contends with a foolish man,
Whether *the fool* rages or laughs, *there is* no peace.

¹⁰ The bloodthirsty hate the blameless,
But the upright seek his well-being.[a]

¹¹ A fool vents all his feelings,[b]
But a wise *man* holds them back.

¹² If a ruler pays attention to lies,
All his servants *become* wicked.

¹³ The poor *man* and the oppressor have this in common:
The LORD gives light to the eyes of both.

Day 186

Acts 8 (New King James Version)

18 And when Simon saw that through the laying on of the apostles' hands the Holy Spirit was given, he offered them money, 19 saying, "Give me this power also, that anyone on whom I lay hands may receive the Holy Spirit."

My thoughts about these verses

_____
_____
_____
_____

20 But Peter said to him, "Your money perish with you, because you thought that the gift of God could be purchased with money! 21 You have neither part nor portion in this matter, for your heart is not right in the sight of God. 22 Repent therefore of this your wickedness, and pray God if perhaps the thought of your heart may be forgiven you. 23 For I see that you are poisoned by bitterness and bound by iniquity."

My thoughts about these verses

_____
_____
_____
_____

24 Then Simon answered and said, "Pray to the Lord for me, that none of the things which you have spoken may come upon me."

Why do you think Simon wanted this type of power?

_____
_____
_____
_____
_____
_____

Day 187

Name the Books of the Bible. Attempt to write them without the use of your Bible to see how much you remember.

1.	40.
2.	41.
3.	42.
4.	43.
5.	44.
6.	45.
7.	46.
8.	47.
9.	48.
10.	49.
11.	50.
12.	51.
13.	52.
14.	53.
15.	54.
16.	55.
17.	56.
18.	57.
19.	58.
20.	59.
21.	60.
22.	61.
23.	62.
24.	63.
25.	64.
26.	65.
27.	66.
28.	
29.	
30.	
31.	
32.	
33.	
34.	
35.	
36.	
37.	
38.	

Day 188

Numbers 30 (New King James Version)

Then Moses spoke to the heads of the tribes concerning the children of Israel, saying, "This is the thing which the LORD has commanded: ² If a man makes a vow to the LORD, or swears an oath to bind himself by some agreement, he shall not break his word; he shall do according to all that proceeds out of his mouth.

With this verse in mine, what will you promise the Lord today?

_____
_____
_____
_____
_____
_____

Do you feel when you pray, providing the prayers are in God's will, that He will bless you with what you asked for?

_____
_____

So if you expect God to keep up His end of the deal, why are you constantly not holding up you end?

_____
_____
_____

Do you just avoid making any promises to God so you don't have to worry about breaking them? Why?

_____
_____
_____
_____
_____

Day 189

The Book of Titus

In Titus 1, what were the qualifications of a Bishop?

_____

_____

_____

In Titus 2, what were the qualities of a sound church?

_____

_____

_____

_____

In Titus 3, finish these verses

*⁹ But avoid foolish*_____

_____.

*¹⁰ Reject*_____

_____ ,

¹¹ knowing _____

_____.

In Titus 1, Paul said that God who could not _____ , promised what before time began? _____

Remind them to be subject to rulers and authorities, to obey, to be ready for every good work, ² to speak evil of no one, to be peaceable, gentle, showing all humility to all men. ³ For we ourselves were also once foolish, disobedient, deceived, serving various lusts and pleasures, living in malice and envy, hateful and hating one another

My thoughts about these verses

_____

_____

_____

Day 190

Titus 1 (New King James Version)

⁵ For this reason I left you in Crete, that you should set in order the things that are lacking, and appoint elders in every city as I commanded you— ⁶ if a man is blameless, the husband of one wife, having faithful children not accused of dissipation or insubordination. ⁷ For a bishop[b] must be blameless, as a steward of God, not self-willed, not quick-tempered, not given to wine, not violent, not greedy for money, ⁸ but hospitable, a lover of what is good, sober-minded, just, holy, self-controlled, ⁹ holding fast the faithful word as he has been taught, that he may be able, by sound doctrine, both to exhort and convict those who contradict.

My thoughts about these verses

_____
_____
_____
_____
_____

How strict are you when it comes to following someone who is a leader in the church?

_____
_____
_____
_____
_____

But, if the bible tells us that every man falls short, how can we hold others to higher standards than we have for ourselves?

_____
_____
_____
_____
_____
_____
_____

Day 191

Hosea 3 (New King James Version)

Then the LORD said to me, "Go again, love a woman who is loved by a lover[a] and is committing adultery, just like the love of the LORD for the children of Israel, who look to other gods and love the raisin cakes of the pagans."

My thoughts about this scripture

_____
_____
_____

Who was Hosea?

_____
_____

What did God instruct Hosea to name his first Daughter?

_____

Why?

_____
_____

[4] For the children of Israel shall abide many days without king or prince, without sacrifice or sacred pillar, without ephod or teraphim. [5] Afterward the children of Israel shall return and seek the LORD their God and David their king. They shall fear the LORD and His goodness in the latter days.

My thoughts about this scripture

_____
_____
_____
_____
_____

Day 192

What will you do today to show God you love Him?
_____
_____

What was have you developed to worship God?
_____
_____
_____

Do you pray throughout the day, praising and thanking God?
_____
_____
_____

Do you pray for your friends and enemies during your day?
_____
_____

Are you getting more comfortable openly expressing you love for Christ?
_____
_____

Can you name the first, fifth and nineteenth books of the Bible?
_____, _____, _____.

May God continue to bless you.

Day 193

Genesis 45 (New King James Version)

³ Then Joseph said to his brothers, "I am Joseph; does my father still live?" But his brothers could not answer him, for they were dismayed in his presence. ⁴ And Joseph said to his brothers, "Please come near to me." So they came near. Then he said: "I am Joseph your brother, whom you sold into Egypt. ⁵ But now, do not therefore be grieved or angry with yourselves because you sold me here; for God sent me before you to preserve life. ⁶ For these two years the famine has been in the land, and there are still five years in which there will be neither plowing nor harvesting. ⁷ And God sent me before you to preserve a posterity for you in the earth, and to save your lives by a great deliverance. ⁸ So now it was not you who sent me here, but God; and He has made me a father to Pharaoh, and lord of all his house, and a ruler throughout all the land of Egypt.

My thoughts about this scripture

_____

_____

_____

_____

_____

_____

Do you believe God can take what someone meant as evil towards you and turn it into good?

_____

_____

Write about a time when you knew someone tried to hurt you but God worked it out in your favor.

_____

_____

_____

_____

_____

_____

_____

_____

_____

_____

_____

Day 194

Matthew 23 (New King James Version)

Then Jesus spoke to the multitudes and to His disciples, [2] saying: "The scribes and the Pharisees sit in Moses' seat. [3] Therefore whatever they tell you to observe,[a] that observe and do, but do not do according to their works; for they say, and do not do. [4] For they bind heavy burdens, hard to bear, and lay them on men's shoulders; but they themselves will not move them with one of their fingers. [5] But all their works they do to be seen by men. They make their phylacteries broad and enlarge the borders of their garments. [6] They love the best places at feasts, the best seats in the synagogues, [7] greetings in the marketplaces, and to be called by men, 'Rabbi, Rabbi.' [8] But you, do not be called 'Rabbi'; for One is your Teacher, the Christ,[b] and you are all brethren. [9] Do not call anyone on earth your father; for One is your Father, He who is in heaven. [10] And do not be called teachers; for One is your Teacher, the Christ. [11] But he who is greatest among you shall be your servant. [12] And whoever exalts himself will be humbled, and he who humbles himself will be exalted.

Do you experience any people now who can tell you what to do to be a good Christian but they do something else?

_____

_____

_____

How do you handle them?

_____

_____

_____

Do you try to "practice what you preach"?

_____

_____

_____

How do you humble yourself daily?

_____

_____

_____

_____

Day 195

Psalm 23 (New King James Version)

The LORD is my shepherd;
I shall not want.
² He makes me to lie down in green pastures;
He leads me beside the still waters.
³ He restores my soul;
He leads me in the paths of righteousness
For His name's sake.

Psalm 25 (New King James Version)

To You, O LORD, I lift up my soul.
² O my God, I trust in You;
Let me not be ashamed;
Let not my enemies triumph over me.
³ Indeed, let no one who waits on You be ashamed;
Let those be ashamed who deal treacherously without cause.

Psalm 144 (New King James Version)

¹¹ Rescue me and deliver me from the hand of foreigners,
Whose mouth speaks lying words,
And whose right hand is a right hand of falsehood—
¹² That our sons may be as plants grown up in their youth;
That our daughters may be as pillars,
Sculptured in palace style;

My thoughts about these verses

_____

_____

_____

_____

_____

_____

Day 196

Galatians 6 (New King James Version)

Brethren, if a man is overtaken in any trespass, you who are spiritual restore such a one in a spirit of gentleness, considering yourself lest you also be tempted. [2] Bear one another's burdens, and so fulfill the law of Christ. [3] For if anyone thinks himself to be something, when he is nothing, he deceives himself. [4] But let each one examine his own work, and then he will have rejoicing in himself alone, and not in another. [5] For each one shall bear his own load.

My thoughts about this scripture

_____
_____
_____
_____
_____

Do you try to help someone when they are losing faith?

_____
_____

Do you sometimes feel your level of Christianity is too high to help bear the burden of new Christians? Explain Yes or No

_____
_____
_____
_____
_____

Day 197

Joshua 7 (New King James Version)

*¹⁰ So the L*ORD *said to Joshua: "Get up! Why do you lie thus on your face?* *¹¹*
*Israel has sinned, and they have also transgressed My covenant which I
commanded them. For they have even taken some of the accursed things, and
have both stolen and deceived; and they have also put it among their own stuff.*
*¹² Therefore the children of Israel could not stand before their enemies, but
turned their backs before their enemies, because they have become doomed to
destruction. Neither will I be with you anymore, unless you destroy the accursed
from among you.* *¹³ Get up, sanctify the people, and say, 'Sanctify yourselves for
tomorrow, because thus says the L*ORD *God of Israel: "There is an accursed
thing in your midst, O Israel; you cannot stand before your enemies until you
take away the accursed thing from among you."*

ac·curs·ed (-kûr s d, -kûrst) also ac·curst (-kûrst). adj. 1. Abominable;
hateful: this **accursed** mud. 2. Being under a curse; doomed.

Do you ask God to provide things for you that are not of God?

_____

_____

❖ Have you ever asked God for someone else's spouse?

❖ Prayed someone ill or even dead so you could have their position?

❖ Prayed for wealth and power so you could sleep around, do drugs
and treat people poorly?

Don't you think having those "accursed" feelings and thoughts removed should
be the basis of all your prayers? Why or Why not?

_____
_____
_____
_____
_____
_____
_____
_____

Day 198

Matthew 26 (New King James Version)

14 Then one of the twelve, called Judas Iscariot, went to the chief priests 15 and said, "What are you willing to give me if I deliver Him to you?" And they counted out to him thirty pieces of silver. 16 So from that time he sought opportunity to betray Him.

My thoughts about this scripture

_____
_____
_____
_____
_____

Do you know what Judas was prior to following Jesus?

_____
_____

How did Judas make known to the Priest and the Guards who Jesus was when they came for Him?

_____
_____

After betraying Jesus, how does Judas deal with it?

_____
_____
_____

Day 199

Complete the following;

Matthew 27 (New King James Version)

[35] Then they crucified Him, and divided His garments, casting lots,[f] that it might be fulfilled which was spoken by the prophet:
"They divided _____
_____".

[45] *Now from the sixth hour until the ninth hour there was darkness over all the land.* [46] *And about the ninth hour Jesus cried out with a loud voice, saying, "Eli, Eli, lama sabachthani?"*

_____
_____?"

[54] *So when the centurion and those with him, who were guarding Jesus, saw the earthquake and the things that had happened, they feared greatly, saying,*
"_____!"

Day 200

You have spent 200 days getting closer to Christ. Below write the changes you've noticed about you and your way of dealing with things differently. Also write new things you've learned about the Bible, God's word and about yourself during this time. Remember, be honest. Even if you only note small changes, they are changes and we all have to start somewhere. Keep working, keep praying and keep believing in Christ.

God Bless you!!

My Changes

_____
_____
_____
_____
_____
_____
_____
_____
_____
_____

New things I've learned

_____
_____
_____
_____
_____
_____
_____
_____
_____

Day 201

Deuteronomy 4 (New King James Version)

"Now, O Israel, listen to the statutes and the judgments which I teach you to observe, that you may live, and go in and possess the land which the LORD God of your fathers is giving you. ² You shall not add to the word which I command you, nor take from it, that you may keep the commandments of the LORD your God which I command you. ³ Your eyes have seen what the LORD did at Baal Peor; for the LORD your God has destroyed from among you all the men who followed Baal of Peor. ⁴ But you who held fast to the LORD your God are alive today, every one of you.

My thoughts about this scripture

_____
_____
_____
_____
_____
_____

Find verses 5-6 and write them below

_____
_____
_____
_____
_____
_____
_____

My thoughts about verses 5-6

_____
_____
_____
_____
_____
_____
_____
_____

Day 202

Songs of Praise

```
D  M  H  T  F  S  G  W  D  S  E  V  A  C  B
E  O  I  B  H  G  U  E  P  M  U  U  F  I  R
S  K  L  H  U  E  W  P  E  A  T  H  N  F  I
S  W  M  R  Y  F  Y  N  E  H  N  T  S  S  G
E  Y  X  N  I  F  I  T  E  R  H  X  W  U  H
L  V  W  D  W  G  I  B  H  E  S  K  I  S  T
B  H  N  S  A  K  L  R  M  A  V  T  P  E  E
E  A  X  M  Y  O  F  I  O  P  T  I  A  J  R
B  N  I  A  O  X  D  X  W  L  B  W  M  R  D
C  U  F  D  V  D  A  E  P  R  G  E  A  Q  A
S  U  R  E  L  G  O  O  D  N  E  S  S  I  Y
P  S  Y  E  N  W  O  D  W  O  B  W  D  U  T
I  R  Q  R  W  U  F  I  A  D  A  P  S  N  H
S  R  O  R  E  U  Q  N  O  C  V  L  F  N  M
R  E  L  E  T  I  T  R  A  I  N  N  K  U  A
```

AND I
BOW DOWN
GLORIFY HIM
JESUS
SUREL GOODNESS

ANSWER
BRIGHTER DAY
IMAGINE ME
LET IT RAIN
THE BLOOD

BE BLESSED
CONQUERORS
IN THE MIDDLE
SUPERSTAR
THEY THAT WAIT

Day 203

Micah 3 (New King James Version)

[4] Then they will cry to the LORD,
But He will not hear them;
He will even hide His face from them at that time,
Because they have been evil in their deeds.

My thoughts about this scripture

_____
_____
_____
_____
_____

Are you obedient when you want things but in total disobedience when things are going well?

_____
_____
_____

Do you believe that even if you get things being disobedient you may be erasing your name from Heaven's Holy Book?

_____
_____
_____
_____
_____

Day 204

Genesis 41 (New King James Version)

15 And Pharaoh said to Joseph, "I have had a dream, and there is no one who can interpret it. But I have heard it said of you that you can understand a dream, to interpret it."

16 So Joseph answered Pharaoh, saying, "It is not in me; God will give Pharaoh an answer of peace."

25 Then Joseph said to Pharaoh, "The dreams of Pharaoh are one; God has shown Pharaoh what He is about to do

My thoughts about this scripture

_____
_____
_____
_____
_____
_____
_____

Why do you believe Joseph never used this opportunity to make this about him?

_____
_____
_____
_____
_____
_____

Genesis 41 (New King James Version)

38 And Pharaoh said to his servants, "Can we find such a one as this, a man in whom is the Spirit of God?"

39 Then Pharaoh said to Joseph, "Inasmuch as God has shown you all this, there is no one as discerning and wise as you. 40 You shall be over my house, and all my people shall be ruled according to your word; only in regard to the throne will I be greater than you." 41 And Pharaoh said to Joseph, "See, I have set you over all the land of Egypt."

My thoughts about this scripture

_____
_____
_____
_____
_____

Write a few of the bad things Joseph had to endure before reaching Pharaoh.

_____
_____
_____
_____
_____
_____
_____

Day 206

2 Samuel 23 (New King James Version)

*² "The Spirit of the L*ORD *spoke by me,*
And His word was on my tongue.
³ The God of Israel said,
The Rock of Israel spoke to me:
'He who rules over men must be just,
Ruling in the fear of God.
⁴ And he shall be like the light of the morning when the sun rises,
A morning without clouds,
Like the tender grass springing out of the earth,
By clear shining after rain.'

My thoughts about this scripture

_____
_____
_____
_____
_____
_____

How do you lead the people who follow you? (family, friends, children)

_____
_____
_____

Do you think being rude and disrespectful is necessary in order for certain people to follow the rules?

_____
_____
_____
_____

Day 207

Jeremiah 8 (New King James Version)

17 "For behold, I will send serpents among you,
Vipers which cannot be charmed,
And they shall bite you," says the LORD.

Why have they provoked Me to anger
With their carved images—
With foreign idols?"

20 "The harvest is past,
The summer is ended,
And we are not saved!"

13 "I will surely consume them," says the LORD.
"No grapes shall be on the vine,
Nor figs on the fig tree,
And the leaf shall fade;
And the things I have given them shall pass away from them.""

My thoughts about these verses

_____
_____
_____
_____
_____

Do you believe you can continue to be disobedient and God not do anything?

_____
_____
_____
_____
_____

Day 208

Ezekiel 44 (New King James Version)

⁶ "Now say to the rebellious, to the house of Israel, 'Thus says the Lord GOD: "O house of Israel, let Us have no more of all your abominations. ⁷ When you brought in foreigners, uncircumcised in heart and uncircumcised in flesh, to be in My sanctuary to defile it—My house—and when you offered My food, the fat and the blood, then they broke My covenant because of all your abominations. ⁸ And you have not kept charge of My holy things, but you have set others to keep charge of My sanctuary for you." ⁹ Thus says the Lord GOD: "No foreigner, uncircumcised in heart or uncircumcised in flesh, shall enter My sanctuary, including any foreigner who is among the children of Israel.

My thoughts about this scripture

_____
_____
_____
_____
_____
_____
_____

What do you think is meant by "foreigner"?

_____
_____
_____
_____
_____

What do you think is meant by "you have set others to keep charge of My sanctuary"?

_____
_____
_____
_____
_____

Day 209

John 4 (New King James Version)

⁹ Then the woman of Samaria said to Him, "How is it that You, being a Jew, ask a drink from me, a Samaritan woman?" For Jews have no dealings with Samaritans.

¹⁰ Jesus answered and said to her, "If you knew the gift of God, and who it is who says to you, 'Give Me a drink,' you would have asked Him, and He would have given you living water."

¹¹ The woman said to Him, "Sir, You have nothing to draw with, and the well is deep. Where then do You get that living water? ¹² Are You greater than our father Jacob, who gave us the well, and drank from it himself, as well as his sons and his livestock?"

¹³ Jesus answered and said to her, "Whoever drinks of this water will thirst again, ¹⁴ but whoever drinks of the water that I shall give him will never thirst. But the water that I shall give him will become in him a fountain of water springing up into everlasting life."

My thoughts about these verses

_____
_____
_____
_____
_____
_____
_____

Why do you think it was important to mention this was a Samaritan woman?

_____
_____
_____

What is meant by "will never thirst"?

_____
_____
_____

Daily Nourishment

Read and apply these verses to your life today.

Proverbs (New King James Version)

*²³ Whoever guards his mouth and tongue
Keeps his soul from troubles.*

*³⁰ There is no wisdom or understanding
Or counsel against the LORD.*

*¹⁷ Incline your ear and hear the words of the wise,
And apply your heart to my knowledge;*

*⁴ Do not overwork to be rich;
Because of your own understanding, cease!*

*¹³ Do not withhold correction from a child,
For if you beat him with a rod, he will not die.
¹⁴ You shall beat him with a rod,
And deliver his soul from hell.[b]*

Day 211

[14] Now when Jesus had come into Peter's house, He saw his wife's mother lying sick with a fever. [15] So He touched her hand, and the fever left her. And she arose and served them.[a]

[26] But He said to them, "Why are you fearful, O you of little faith?" Then He arose and rebuked the winds and the sea, and there was a great calm. [27] So the men marveled, saying, "Who can this be, that even the winds and the sea obey Him?"

When He had come down from the mountain, great multitudes followed Him. [2] And behold, a leper came and worshiped Him, saying, "Lord, if You are willing, You can make me clean."

[3] Then Jesus put out His hand and touched him, saying, "I am willing; be cleansed." Immediately his leprosy was cleansed.

Do you understand the goodness and the power in the God we serve?

_____
_____
_____
_____
_____

Write a miracle that God has performed in your life.

_____
_____
_____
_____
_____
_____
_____
_____
_____
_____

Matthew 7 (New King James Version)

Judge not, that you be not judged. [2] For with what judgment you judge, you will be judged; and with the measure you use, it will be measured back to you. [3] And why do you look at the speck in your brother's eye, but do not consider the plank in your own eye? [4] Or how can you say to your brother, 'Let me remove the speck from your eye'; and look, a plank is in your own eye? [5] Hypocrite! First remove the plank from your own eye, and then you will see clearly to remove the speck from your brother's eye.

My thoughts about this scripture

_____
_____
_____
_____
_____
_____
_____

What is meant by "*First remove the plank from your own eye, and then you will see clearly to remove the speck from your brother's eye*".

_____
_____
_____
_____
_____
_____
_____

Day 213

Revelation 7 (New King James Version)

⁹ After these things I looked, and behold, a great multitude which no one could number, of all nations, tribes, peoples, and tongues, standing before the throne and before the Lamb, clothed with white robes, with palm branches in their hands, ¹⁰ and crying out with a loud voice, saying, "Salvation belongs to our God who sits on the throne, and to the Lamb!" ¹¹ All the angels stood around the throne and the elders and the four living creatures, and fell on their faces before the throne and worshiped God, ¹² saying:

"Amen! Blessing and glory and wisdom,
Thanksgiving and honor and power and might,
Be to our God forever and ever.
Amen."

My thoughts about this scripture

_____
_____
_____
_____
_____
_____
_____

There is a song that says "I want to be in that number". As a child of God, write what it means to know you will be in that number

_____
_____
_____
_____
_____
_____
_____
_____
_____
_____

Day 214

Deuteronomy 30 (New King James Version)

[7] *"Also the LORD your God will put all these curses on your enemies and on those who hate you, who persecuted you. [8] And you will again obey the voice of the LORD and do all His commandments which I command you today. [9] The LORD your God will make you abound in all the work of your hand, in the fruit of your body, in the increase of your livestock, and in the produce of your land for good. For the LORD will again rejoice over you for good as He rejoiced over your fathers, [10] if you obey the voice of the LORD your God, to keep His commandments and His statutes which are written in this Book of the Law, and if you turn to the LORD your God with all your heart and with all your soul*

My thoughts about this scripture

_____
_____
_____
_____
_____
_____

If all good things are promised to those who obey the LORD and keep His commandments, why do people continue to be disobedient?

_____
_____
_____
_____
_____
_____
_____

Day 215

Judges 11 (New King James Version)

²⁹ Then the Spirit of the Lord came upon Jephthah, and he passed through Gilead and Manasseh, and passed through Mizpah of Gilead; and from Mizpah of Gilead he advanced toward the people of Ammon. ³⁰ And Jephthah made a vow to the Lord, and said, "If You will indeed deliver the people of Ammon into my hands, ³¹ then it will be that whatever comes out of the doors of my house to meet me, when I return in peace from the people of Ammon, shall surely be the Lord's, and I will offer it up as a burnt offering."

My thoughts about this scripture

_____
_____
_____
_____
_____
_____

Do you think our earthy desires cause us to offer God more than we are willing to deliver?

_____
_____
_____
_____

The Bible tells us that when you make a promise to God, he expects us to deliver. Knowing this, are you more careful what promises you make?

_____
_____

Day 216

James 2:5 (New King James Version)

⁵ Listen, my beloved brethren: Has God not chosen the poor of this world to be rich in faith and heirs of the kingdom which He promised to those who love Him?

You may not believe this but we have more when we have faith than when we have stuff. Again, it is hard to believe but if we have faith we will eventually have stuff. We just have to have patience and be faithful.

I agree because

_____
_____
_____

I disagree because

_____
_____
_____

My thoughts about this scripture

_____
_____
_____
_____
_____
_____
_____
_____

Day 217

Matthew 10 (New King James Version)

27 "Whatever I tell you in the dark, speak in the light; and what you hear in the ear, preach on the housetops. 28 And do not fear those who kill the body but cannot kill the soul. But rather fear Him who is able to destroy both soul and body in hell. 29 Are not two sparrows sold for a copper coin? And not one of them falls to the ground apart from your Father's will. 30 But the very hairs of your head are all numbered. 31 Do not fear therefore; you are of more value than many sparrows.

My thoughts about this scripture

_____
_____
_____
_____
_____
_____
_____
_____

Do you find yourself in fear of everyone except God?

_____

Do you believe God has the ability to both protect and destroy you?

_____
_____
_____

Please express why you fear man

_____
_____
_____
_____

Day 218

Matthew 10 (New King James Version)

⁴⁰ "He who receives you receives Me, and he who receives Me receives Him who sent Me. ⁴¹ He who receives a prophet in the name of a prophet shall receive a prophet's reward. And he who receives a righteous man in the name of a righteous man shall receive a righteous man's reward. ⁴² And whoever gives one of these little ones only a cup of cold water in the name of a disciple, assuredly, I say to you, he shall by no means lose his reward."

Do you help others with a cheerful heart?

_____
_____
_____
_____

Have you ever been upset when you knew God was directing you to do something you didn't want to do?

_____
_____
_____
_____

What I thought when I read this scripture

_____
_____
_____
_____
_____
_____
_____
_____
_____

Day 219

Luke 8 (New King James Version)

Now it came to pass, afterward, that He went through every city and village, preaching and bringing the glad tidings of the kingdom of God. And the twelve were with Him, [2] *and certain women who had been healed of evil spirits and infirmities—Mary called Magdalene, out of whom had come seven demons,* [3] *and Joanna the wife of Chuza, Herod's steward, and Susanna, and many others who provided for Him[a] from their substance.*

My thoughts about this scripture

_____
_____
_____
_____
_____
_____
_____
_____

Does the fact that the Bible mentions these women had demons removed from them remind you of people's testimonies today?

_____
_____
_____
_____

Day 220

Review

1. How many Books are there in the Old Testament? _____
2. How many Books are there in the New Testament? _____
3. What was the name of the woman God gave Adam? _____
4. The name of the Book where Paul writes to the people of Colosse?
   _____
5. What did Paul do before becoming a disciple? _____
6. Name one of the Twelve. _____
7. Who was Solomon's father? _____
8. Genesis talks about God creating what? _____
9. What book & verse will you find this "*For God so loved the world that He gave His only begotten Son, that whoever believes in Him should not perish but have everlasting life.* _____

10. What was the name of the richest King? _____

Complete the following;

1. [24] And again I say to you, _____
   _____
   _____.

   (Matthew 19:24)

2. *In the beginning God* _____
   _____
   _____

   (Genesis 1:1-2)

3. Write your favorite scripture here.

   _____
   _____
   _____
   _____

Day 221

1 Peter 2 (New King James Version)

Therefore, laying aside all malice, all deceit, hypocrisy, envy, and all evil speaking, [2] as newborn babes, desire the pure milk of the word, that you may grow thereby,[a] [3] if indeed you have tasted that the Lord is gracious.

My thoughts about this scripture

_____
_____
_____
_____
_____
_____
_____

Why do you think God's word is compared to milk for a newborn baby?

_____
_____
_____
_____
_____
_____
_____
_____

Day 222

1 Peter 2 (New King James Version)

¹³ Therefore submit yourselves to every ordinance of man for the Lord's sake, whether to the king as supreme, ¹⁴ or to governors, as to those who are sent by him for the punishment of evildoers and for the praise of those who do good. ¹⁵ For this is the will of God, that by doing good you may put to silence the ignorance of foolish men— ¹⁶ as free, yet not using liberty as a cloak for vice, but as bondservants of God. ¹⁷ Honor all people. Love the brotherhood. Fear God. Honor the king.

My thoughts about this scripture

_____
_____
_____
_____
_____
_____
_____

What does this mean about elective officials? (Even the ones you didn't vote for)

_____
_____
_____
_____
_____

Day 223

Find the following verses and write them below

1. 1 Chronicles 23:2-3

_____
_____
_____
_____
_____
_____

2. Deuteronomy 18:9-10

_____
_____
_____
_____
_____
_____

3. Revelation 9:3-6

_____
_____
_____
_____
_____
_____
_____
_____
_____
_____
_____
_____
_____

Day 224

Revelation 12 (New King James Version)

[7] And war broke out in heaven: Michael and his angels fought with the dragon; and the dragon and his angels fought, [8] but they did not prevail, nor was a place found for them[a] in heaven any longer. [9] So the great dragon was cast out, that serpent of old, called the Devil and Satan, who deceives the whole world; he was cast to the earth, and his angels were cast out with him.

My thoughts about this scripture

_____
_____
_____
_____
_____
_____
_____
_____

The scripture says that Satan deceives the whole world. What steps have you taken to ensure you are not repeatedly deceived the same way by him?

_____
_____
_____
_____
_____
_____
_____
_____
_____
_____
_____
_____

Complete the following

Zephaniah 2 (New King James Version)

Gather yourselves together, yes, gather together,
O undesirable[a] nation,
² Before the decree is _____

_____
_____!

Ruth 3 (New King James Version)

⁶ So she went down

_____
_____.

⁷ And after Boaz had eaten and drunk,

_____
_____
_____.

Write a scripture you can remember here. (Get as close as you can before looking)

_____
_____
_____
_____
_____
_____

Day 226

Obadiah 1 (New King James Version)

12 *"But you should not have gazed on the day of your brother*
In the day of his captivity;[b]
Nor should you have rejoiced over the children of Judah
In the day of their destruction;
Nor should you have spoken proudly
In the day of distress.
13 *You should not have entered the gate of My people*
In the day of their calamity.
Indeed, you should not have gazed on their affliction
In the day of their calamity,
Nor laid hands on their substance
In the day of their calamity.
14 *You should not have stood at the crossroads*
To cut off those among them who escaped;
Nor should you have delivered up those among them who remained
In the day of distress.

My thoughts about this scripture

_____
_____
_____
_____
_____
_____
_____

Do you put others down when they are going through hard times? Why or why not?

_____
_____
_____
_____
_____
_____

Job 31 (New King James Version)

"I have made a covenant with my eyes;
Why then should I look upon a young woman?
² For what is the allotment of God from above,
And the inheritance of the Almighty from on high?
³ Is it not destruction for the wicked,
And disaster for the workers of iniquity?
⁴ Does He not see my ways,
And count all my steps?

My thoughts about this scripture

_____
_____
_____
_____
_____

²⁹ "If I have rejoiced at the destruction of him who hated me,
Or lifted myself up when evil found him
³⁰ (Indeed I have not allowed my mouth to sin
By asking for a curse on his soul);

My thoughts about this scripture

_____
_____
_____
_____
_____
_____

Day 228

Put a little Love in your heart today.

Jesus said to them, "If God were your Father, you would love Me, for I proceeded forth and came from God; nor have I come of Myself, but He sent Me.

for they loved the praise of men more than the praise of God.

"If you love Me, keep My commandments.

Now hope does not disappoint, because the love of God has been poured out in our hearts by the Holy Spirit who was given to us.

Husbands, love your wives and do not be bitter toward them.

Now may the Lord direct your hearts into the love of God and into the patience of Christ.

And now I plead with you, lady, not as though I wrote a new commandment to you, but that which we have had from the beginning: that we love one another.

Psalm 3 (New King James Version)

LORD, how they have increased who trouble me!
Many are they who rise up against me.
² Many are they who say of me,
"There is no help for him in God." Selah

³ But You, O LORD, are a shield for me,
My glory and the One who lifts up my head.
⁴ I cried to the LORD with my voice,
And He heard me from His holy hill. Selah

⁵ I lay down and slept;
I awoke, for the LORD sustained me.
⁶ I will not be afraid of ten thousands of people
Who have set themselves against me all around.

⁷ Arise, O LORD;
Save me, O my God!
For You have struck all my enemies on the cheekbone;
You have broken the teeth of the ungodly.
⁸ Salvation belongs to the LORD.
Your blessing is upon Your people. Selah

My thoughts about this scripture

_____
_____
_____
_____
_____
_____
_____
_____

(I researched the word "Selah" and there were so many confusing definitions for it, I decided not to give one.)

The Book of John

1. Which disciple often referred to himself as "The one that Jesus Loved"?
    A. Paul
    B. Peter
    C. John
    D. Judas

2. When John was asked who he was he answered

    _____

    _____

    (John 1:23)

3. When Jesus said "Behold, and Israelite indeed, in whom is no deceit". Who was He referring to? (John 1:47)
    A. Nathanael
    B. Moses
    C. John
    D. Philip

4. When Jesus turned water into wine, they were attending _____.
    A. A Funeral
    B. A Wedding
    C. A Church Service
    D. A Jewish baptism

5. The Book of John comes right before _____
    A. Luke
    B. Mark
    C. Matthew
    D. Acts

Day 231

Matthew 5 (New King James Version)

³ "Blessed are the poor in spirit,
For theirs is the kingdom of heaven.
⁴ Blessed are those who mourn,
For they shall be comforted.
⁵ Blessed are the meek,
For they shall inherit the earth.
⁶ Blessed are those who hunger and thirst for righteousness,
For they shall be filled.
⁷ Blessed are the merciful,
For they shall obtain mercy.
⁸ Blessed are the pure in heart,
For they shall see God.
⁹ Blessed are the peacemakers,
For they shall be called sons of God.
¹⁰ Blessed are those who are persecuted for righteousness' sake,
For theirs is the kingdom of heaven.

My thoughts about this scripture

_____
_____
_____
_____
_____
_____
_____
_____

After reading this, are you blessed?

_____
_____

Day 232

Matthew 18 (New King James Version)

[6] *"Whoever causes one of these little ones who believe in Me to sin, it would be better for him if a millstone were hung around his neck, and he were drowned in the depth of the sea. [7] Woe to the world because of offenses! For offenses must come, but woe to that man by whom the offense comes!*

[8] *"If your hand or foot causes you to sin, cut it off and cast it from you. It is better for you to enter into life lame or maimed, rather than having two hands or two feet, to be cast into the everlasting fire. [9] And if your eye causes you to sin, pluck it out and cast it from you. It is better for you to enter into life with one eye, rather than having two eyes, to be cast into hell fire.*

My thoughts about this scripture

_____
_____
_____
_____
_____
_____

Even if you are not ready to believe or trust in God, are you making sure you aren't pushing anyone else away as well?

_____
_____
_____

Day 233

Deuteronomy 2 (New King James Version)

2 "And the LORD spoke to me, saying: 3 'You have skirted this mountain long enough; turn northward. 4 And command the people, saying, "You are about to pass through the territory of your brethren, the descendants of Esau, who live in Seir; and they will be afraid of you. Therefore watch yourselves carefully. 5 Do not meddle with them, for I will not give you any of their land, no, not so much as one footstep, because I have given Mount Seir to Esau as a possession. 6 You shall buy food from them with money, that you may eat; and you shall also buy water from them with money, that you may drink.

My thoughts about this scripture

_____
_____
_____
_____
_____
_____
_____

Do you believe that God has certain things for certain people?

_____

If so, do you believe that when you try to take or "meddle" with things he has for others it usually doesn't work out for you? Explain.

_____
_____
_____
_____
_____
_____
_____

Day 234

THE TWELVE

```
K  T  V  R  U  I  C  B  B  W  F  L  X  M  P
Q  Q  Q  H  B  X  K  A  L  U  E  O  E  E  N
O  V  Q  L  L  O  O  R  J  U  I  R  V  C  G
F  R  D  J  H  O  O  T  C  M  A  B  D  G  D
W  P  M  M  F  R  J  H  F  E  M  W  L  N  A
C  V  E  W  H  U  S  O  L  V  K  E  J  J  A
W  E  H  T  T  A  M  L  M  G  B  U  C  R  L
Z  G  I  R  E  E  L  O  W  B  D  S  S  D  H
H  Z  W  W  R  R  P  M  A  A  A  Y  B  C  P
P  K  O  X  F  M  P  E  S  M  J  E  S  R  N
I  H  A  A  X  B  U  W  O  C  A  U  W  W  F
L  F  K  Z  Q  S  Q  H  K  O  M  L  T  L  I
I  U  I  F  V  E  T  W  X  Z  E  N  H  O  J
H  C  V  B  V  B  V  O  F  Q  S  H  W  G  U
P  S  I  M  O  N  I  Q  R  P  R  H  P  F  E
```

ANDREW	BARTHOLOMEW	JAMES
JOHN	JUDAS	LEBBAEUS
MATTHEW	PETER	PHILIP
SIMON	THOMAS	

Day 235

Margie had just retired from a factory job two months ago and she was beginning to become restless. She spoke with a friend who had retired a year earlier to get some ideas of what she could do to help pass the time. Her friend mentioned helping at a shelter, a group home or a food bank. Margie thought that was a great idea. She made a few calls and met with the directors of a local homeless shelter. They asked if she could come by two days per week and help serve food. Margie was excited that she would have something to do plus she was truly excited about helping people.

After no time at all the regulars who visited the shelter came to know and love Margie. She knew many of them by name and would sometimes sneak them a little snack to take with them.

One afternoon as they were cleaning up, the director and an employee walked up to Margie with huge smiles on their faces. "Congratulations"! The yelled, "you've made it one year today Margie", the director said. Two other volunteers came from the kitchen with a cake with one white candle in the middle of it. They all hugged Margie and thanked her for the great work she provided for the shelter.

The director handed Margie a card which read, "There is a place for you in our hearts as well as a place for you in Heaven". Margie smiled and said thank you. The director could tell there was something wrong. *"Are you okay?"* she asked. *"Yes, I'm fine,* Margie responded. *"It's just...well never mind". "It's just what, please tell us"*, one of the volunteers said. *"Well, I don't really believe in Heaven or Hell or even God for that matter"*, Margie said. They all were shocked. How could someone so giving, so caring, someone filled with so much love not believe in God, they wondered.

"I'm sorry", the director said. *"I was sure you were saved. If someone had asked me, I would have said you were one of the best Christians I know"*, the director added. *"I get that a lot, I really like to help people but I was never introduced to God. I just assumed if I did things the right way if there was a God and a Heaven I would end up there somehow"*, Margie said with her head down. Brenda, one of the volunteers spoke up. *"No, Margie. I'm sorry it doesn't work that way. You have to confess with your mouth that Jesus Christ died on the cross for your sins and that he rose again on the third day" "Once you confess it with your mouth you have to believe it in your heart"*, Brenda continued. *"How can I believe in something I know nothing about?"* Margie asked. *"What are you doing Sunday"*, Brenda asked as she grabbed Margie's hand. *"I think going to church with you,"* Marie said smiling and squeezing Brenda's hand. *"Ya got that right*, Brenda said as she smiled back.

Margie attended church with Brenda that Sunday and every Sunday after that. Margie is still helping at the shelter. She is still just as loving and caring the only difference is now she does it for the glory of God.

Day 236

Matthew 10 (New King James Version)

32 "Therefore whoever confesses Me before men, him I will also confess before My Father who is in heaven. 33 But whoever denies Me before men, him I will also deny before My Father who is in heaven.

My thoughts about this scripture

_____
_____
_____
_____
_____

In confessing Jesus before man, do you feel this is just telling people or is there something more?

_____
_____
_____
_____
_____

Can you be a Christian and still deny Jesus?

_____
_____
_____
_____

Day 237

Nehemiah 1 (New King James Version)

[5] *And I said: "I pray, LORD God of heaven, O great and awesome God, You who keep Your covenant and mercy with those who love You[b] and observe Your[c] commandments,* [6] *please let Your ear be attentive and Your eyes open, that You may hear the prayer of Your servant which I pray before You now, day and night, for the children of Israel Your servants, and confess the sins of the children of Israel which we have sinned against You. Both my father's house and I have sinned.* [7] *We have acted very corruptly against You, and have not kept the commandments, the statutes, nor the ordinances which You commanded Your servant Moses.*

My thoughts about this scripture

_____

_____

_____

_____

_____

_____

_____

When you have been disobedient or corrupt, do you confess and pray to God or do you believe that if you don't mention it to Him, He won't know?

_____

_____

_____

_____

_____

_____

_____

_____

Day 238

Psalm 135 (New King James Version)

Praise the LORD!

Praise the name of the LORD;
Praise Him, O you servants of the LORD!
[2] You who stand in the house of the LORD,
In the courts of the house of our God,
[3] Praise the LORD, for the LORD is good;
Sing praises to His name, for it is pleasant.
[4] For the LORD has chosen Jacob for Himself,
Israel for His special treasure.

[5] For I know that the LORD is great,
And our Lord is above all gods.
[6] Whatever the LORD pleases He does,
In heaven and in earth,
In the seas and in all deep places.
[7] He causes the vapors to ascend from the ends of the earth;
He makes lightning for the rain;
He brings the wind out of His treasuries

My thoughts about this scripture

_____
_____
_____
_____
_____
_____

Job 24 (New King James Version)

Since times are not hidden from the Almighty,
Why do those who know Him see not His days?

[2] "Some remove landmarks;
They seize flocks violently and feed on them;
[3] They drive away the donkey of the fatherless;
They take the widow's ox as a pledge.
[4] They push the needy off the road;
All the poor of the land are forced to hide.
[5] Indeed, like wild donkeys in the desert,
They go out to their work, searching for food.
The wilderness yields food for them and for their children.
[6] They gather their fodder in the field
And glean in the vineyard of the wicked.
[7] They spend the night naked, without clothing,
And have no covering in the cold.
[8] They are wet with the showers of the mountains,
And huddle around the rock for want of shelter

My thoughts about this scripture

_____
_____
_____
_____
_____
_____
_____

Day 240

Nehemiah 13 (New King James Version)

On that day they read from the Book of Moses in the hearing of the people, and in it was found written that no Ammonite or Moabite should ever come into the assembly of God, [2] because they had not met the children of Israel with bread and water, but hired Balaam against them to curse them. However, our God turned the curse into a blessing. [3] So it was, when they had heard the Law, that they separated all the mixed multitude from Israel.

My thoughts about this scripture

_____
_____
_____
_____
_____
_____
_____

Talk about when God turned a curse into a blessing for you

_____
_____
_____
_____
_____
_____
_____
_____
_____
_____
_____
_____
_____
_____
_____
_____
_____

Day 241

BE ENCOURAGED IN WHATEVER YOUR DAY BRINGS

Jeremiah 17 (New King James Version)

[7] *"Blessed is the man who trusts in the LORD,*
And whose hope is the LORD.
[8] *For he shall be like a tree planted by the waters,*
Which spreads out its roots by the river,
And will not fear[b] when heat comes;
But its leaf will be green,
And will not be anxious in the year of drought,
Nor will cease from yielding fruit.

Matthew 7 (New King James Version)

[7] *"Ask, and it will be given to you; seek, and you will find; knock, and it will be opened to you.* [8] *For everyone who asks receives, and he who seeks finds, and to him who knocks it will be opened.*

Luke 11 (New King James Version)

[28] *But He said, "More than that, blessed are those who hear the word of God and keep it!"*

Knowing that God loves you and that he will provide you with everything you need, how will you spend your day?
    A. Rejoicing
    B. Loving my neighbors and myself
    C. Spreading God's word
    D. All of the above

Day 242

Ruth 1 (New King James Version)

15 And she said, "Look, your sister-in-law has gone back to her people and to her gods; return after your sister-in-law." 16 But Ruth said:

"Entreat me not to leave you,
Or to turn back from following after you;
For wherever you go, I will go;
And wherever you lodge, I will lodge;
Your people shall be my people,
And your God, my God.
17 Where you die, I will die,
And there will I be buried.
The LORD do so to me, and more also,
If anything but death parts you and me."

My thoughts about this scripture

_____
_____
_____
_____
_____

Since we do not know when we are the most influential to others, should we try to be at our best always?

_____
_____
_____

Or, is it their fault for following you?

_____
_____
_____

Day 243

Matthew 26 (New King James Version)

26 And as they were eating, Jesus took bread, blessed[b] and broke it, and gave it to the disciples and said, "Take, eat; this is My body."

27 Then He took the cup, and gave thanks, and gave it to them, saying, "Drink from it, all of you. 28 For this is My blood of the new[c] covenant, which is shed for many for the remission of sins. 29 But I say to you, I will not drink of this fruit of the vine from now on until that day when I drink it new with you in My Father's kingdom."

30 And when they had sung a hymn, they went out to the Mount of Olives.

My thoughts about this scripture

_____
_____
_____
_____
_____
_____
_____

Do you think that the "bread" and the "wine" symbolizes Jesus conquering our hunger and thirst for God's word?

_____
_____
_____
_____

Day 244

⁶ Your own mouth condemns you, and not I;
Yes, your own lips testify against you.

My thoughts about this verse

_____
_____
_____

⁵ But if our unrighteousness demonstrates the righteousness of God, what shall we say?
Is God unjust who inflicts wrath? (I speak as a man.) ⁶ Certainly not! For then how
will God judge the world?

My thoughts about these verses

_____
_____
_____
_____

Should we consider what we say as well as how we act?

_____

Is it important to be respectful in how we talk about others and how we talk about
ourselves? Explain.

_____
_____
_____
_____
_____
_____
_____
_____

Day 245

Jude 1 (New King James Version)

³ Beloved, while I was very diligent to write to you concerning our common salvation, I found it necessary to write to you exhorting you to contend earnestly for the faith which was once for all delivered to the saints. ⁴ For certain men have crept in unnoticed, who long ago were marked out for this condemnation, ungodly men, who turn the grace of our God into lewdness and deny the only Lord God[b] and our Lord Jesus Christ.

My thoughts about this scripture

_____
_____
_____
_____
_____
_____

What is meant by *"For certain men have crept in unnoticed"*?

_____
_____
_____
_____
_____

Do you believe that if you turn to other gods at anytime, you are still denying God?

_____
_____
_____
_____
_____
_____
_____
_____

Day 246

2 Timothy 2 (New King James Version)

²⁰ But in a great house there are not only vessels of gold and silver, but also of wood and clay, some for honor and some for dishonor. ²¹ Therefore if anyone cleanses himself from the latter, he will be a vessel for honor, sanctified and useful for the Master, prepared for every good work. ²² Flee also youthful lusts; but pursue righteousness, faith, love, peace with those who call on the Lord out of a pure heart. ²³ But avoid foolish and ignorant disputes, knowing that they generate strife. ²⁴ And a servant of the Lord must not quarrel but be gentle to all, able to teach, patient, ²⁵ in humility correcting those who are in opposition, if God perhaps will grant them repentance, so that they may know the truth, ²⁶ and that they may come to their senses and escape the snare of the devil, having been taken captive by him to do his will.

My thoughts about this scripture

_____
_____
_____
_____
_____
_____

Verse 23 is very important, how do you incorporate it into your daily experiences?

_____
_____
_____
_____
_____

Do you believe that even true believers can still be captured by the snare of the devil?

_____
_____
_____
_____
_____
_____

Day 247

Ephesians 5 (New King James Version)

Therefore be imitators of God as dear children. ² And walk in love, as Christ also has loved us and given Himself for us, an offering and a sacrifice to God for a sweet-smelling aroma.

³ But fornication and all uncleanness or covetousness, let it not even be named among you, as is fitting for saints; ⁴ neither filthiness, nor foolish talking, nor coarse jesting, which are not fitting, but rather giving of thanks. ⁵ For this you know,[a] that no fornicator, unclean person, nor covetous man, who is an idolater, has any inheritance in the kingdom of Christ and God. ⁶ Let no one deceive you with empty words, for because of these things the wrath of God comes upon the sons of disobedience. ⁷ Therefore do not be partakers with them.

You know what to do, start writing.

_____
_____
_____
_____
_____
_____
_____
_____

In the flesh if we are told what to do to inherit money or receive an insurance claim and we follow it to the letter. Why can't we follow the directions for our father who promises an inheritance like nothing our hearts could desire?

_____
_____
_____
_____
_____
_____

Day 248

John 11 (New King James Version)

38 Then Jesus, again groaning in Himself, came to the tomb. It was a cave, and a stone lay against it. 39 Jesus said, "Take away the stone."

Martha, the sister of him who was dead, said to Him, "Lord, by this time there is a stench, for he has been dead four days."

40 Jesus said to her, "Did I not say to you that if you would believe you would see the glory of God?" 41 Then they took away the stone from the place where the dead man was lying.[d] And Jesus lifted up His eyes and said, "Father, I thank You that You have heard Me. 42 And I know that You always hear Me, but because of the people who are standing by I said this, that they may believe that You sent Me." 43 Now when He had said these things, He cried with a loud voice, "Lazarus, come forth!" 44 And he who had died came out bound hand and foot with graveclothes, and his face was wrapped with a cloth. Jesus said to them, "Loose him, and let him go."

My thoughts about this scripture

_____
_____
_____
_____
_____
_____
_____

Do you truly believe you can see the glory of God?

_____
_____

Why do you think Jesus waited before going to see Lazarus?

_____
_____
_____
_____
_____
_____
_____
_____

Day 249

Luke 23 (New King James Version)

Then the whole multitude of them arose and led Him to Pilate. [2] And they began to accuse Him, saying, "We found this fellow perverting the[a] nation, and forbidding to pay taxes to Caesar, saying that He Himself is Christ, a King."

[3] Then Pilate asked Him, saying, "Are You the King of the Jews?"

He answered him and said, "It is as you say."

[4] So Pilate said to the chief priests and the crowd, "I find no fault in this Man."

[5] But they were the more fierce, saying, "He stirs up the people, teaching throughout all Judea, beginning from Galilee to this place."

My thoughts about this scripture

_____
_____
_____
_____
_____
_____

Do you feel that even today people still falsely accuse Jesus?

_____
_____
_____
_____
_____
_____
_____

Day 250

Deuteronomy 9 (New King James Version)

⁴ "Do not think in your heart, after the LORD your God has cast them out before you, saying, 'Because of my righteousness the LORD has brought me in to possess this land'; but it is because of the wickedness of these nations that the LORD is driving them out from before you. ⁵ It is not because of your righteousness or the uprightness of your heart that you go in to possess their land, but because of the wickedness of these nations that the LORD your God drives them out from before you, and that He may fulfill the word which the LORD swore to your fathers, to Abraham, Isaac, and Jacob. ⁶ Therefore understand that the LORD your God is not giving you this good land to possess because of your righteousness, for you are a stiff-necked people.

My thoughts about this scripture

_____
_____
_____
_____
_____
_____
_____
_____

Are you sometimes caught up with your greatness and not the greatness of God?

_____
_____
_____
_____
_____
_____
_____
_____
_____
_____

Day 251

Zechariah 7 (New King James Version)

⁴ Then the word of the LORD of hosts came to me, saying, ⁵ "Say to all the people of the land, and to the priests: 'When you fasted and mourned in the fifth and seventh months during those seventy years, did you really fast for Me—for Me? ⁶ When you eat and when you drink, do you not eat and drink for yourselves? ⁷ Should you not have obeyed the words which the LORD proclaimed through the former prophets when Jerusalem and the cities around it were inhabited and prosperous, and the South[d] and the Lowland were inhabited?'"

My thoughts about this scripture

_____
_____
_____
_____
_____
_____
_____

Do you know why you fast?

_____
_____
_____

Do you continue to do it for the Lord during the whole fast or does it become a diet or a contest for you?

_____
_____
_____
_____

Day 252

Acts 12 (New King James Version)

Now about that time Herod the king stretched out his hand to harass some from the church. [2] Then he killed James the brother of John with the sword. [3] And because he saw that it pleased the Jews, he proceeded further to seize Peter also. Now it was during the Days of Unleavened Bread. [4] So when he had arrested him, he put him in prison, and delivered him to four squads of soldiers to keep him, intending to bring him before the people after Passover.

My thoughts about this scripture

_____

_____

_____

_____

_____

[5] Peter was therefore kept in prison, but constant[a] prayer was offered to God for him by the church. [6] And when Herod was about to bring him out, that night Peter was sleeping, bound with two chains between two soldiers; and the guards before the door were keeping the prison. [7] Now behold, an angel of the Lord stood by him, and a light shone in the prison; and he struck Peter on the side and raised him up, saying, "Arise quickly!" And his chains fell off his hands. [8] Then the angel said to him, "Gird yourself and tie on your sandals"; and so he did. And he said to him, "Put on your garment and follow me." [9] So he went out and followed him, and did not know that what was done by the angel was real, but thought he was seeing a vision. [10] When they were past the first and the second guard posts, they came to the iron gate that leads to the city, which opened to them of its own accord; and they went out and went down one street, and immediately the angel departed from him.

My thoughts about this scripture

_____

_____

_____

_____

_____

_____

_____

_____

Day 253

Acts 13 (New King James Version)

Now when they had gone through the island[a] to Paphos, they found a certain sorcerer, a false prophet, a Jew whose name was Bar-Jesus, [7] who was with the proconsul, Sergius Paulus, an intelligent man. This man called for Barnabas and Saul and sought to hear the word of God. [8] But Elymas the sorcerer (for so his name is translated) withstood them, seeking to turn the proconsul away from the faith. [9] Then Saul, who also is called Paul, filled with the Holy Spirit, looked intently at him [10] and said, "O full of all deceit and all fraud, you son of the devil, you enemy of all righteousness, will you not cease perverting the straight ways of the Lord? [11] And now, indeed, the hand of the Lord is upon you, and you shall be blind, not seeing the sun for a time."

And immediately a dark mist fell on him, and he went around seeking someone to lead him by the hand. [12] Then the proconsul believed, when he saw what had been done, being astonished at the teaching of the Lord.

My thoughts about this scripture

_____
_____
_____
_____
_____
_____
_____

Do you fear standing in God's way as He does things in your life or the lives of others, even if you don't agree with what He is doing?

_____
_____
_____
_____
_____
_____
_____
_____
_____

Day 254

Exodus 3 (New King James Version)

13 Then Moses said to God, "Indeed, when I come to the children of Israel and say to them, 'The God of your fathers has sent me to you,' and they say to me, 'What is His name?' what shall I say to them?"

14 And God said to Moses, "I AM WHO I AM." And He said, "Thus you shall say to the children of Israel, 'I AM has sent me to you.'" 15 Moreover God said to Moses, "Thus you shall say to the children of Israel: 'The LORD God of your fathers, the God of Abraham, the God of Isaac, and the God of Jacob, has sent me to you.

My thoughts about this scripture

_____
_____
_____
_____
_____
_____
_____

When you talk to people about God, do you try to explain who He is or what He has done?

_____
_____
_____
_____
_____

Deuteronomy 3 (New King James Version)

²³ "Then I pleaded with the LORD at that time, saying: ²⁴ 'O Lord GOD, You have begun to show Your servant Your greatness and Your mighty hand, for what god *is there* in heaven or on earth who can do *anything* like Your works and Your mighty *deeds?* ²⁵ I pray, let me cross over and see the good land beyond the Jordan, those pleasant mountains, and Lebanon.'

²⁶ "But the LORD was angry with me on your account, and would not listen to me. So the LORD said to me: 'Enough of that! Speak no more to Me of this matter. ²⁷ Go up to the top of Pisgah, and lift your eyes toward the west, the north, the south, and the east; behold *it* with your eyes, for you shall not cross over this Jordan. ²⁸ But command Joshua, and encourage him and strengthen him; for he shall go over before this people, and he shall cause them to inherit the land which you will see.'

²⁹ "So we stayed in the valley opposite Beth Peor.

My thoughts about this scripture

_____
_____
_____
_____
_____
_____

Do you believe that some blessings are not for us but are intended to come through us?

_____
_____
_____
_____
_____
_____

Day 256

Ephesians 6 (New King James Version)

[10] Finally, my brethren, be strong in the Lord and in the power of His might. [11] Put on the whole armor of God, that you may be able to stand against the wiles of the devil. [12] For we do not wrestle against flesh and blood, but against principalities, against powers, against the rulers of the darkness of this age,[c] against spiritual hosts of wickedness in the heavenly places. [13] Therefore take up the whole armor of God, that you may be able to withstand in the evil day, and having done all, to stand.

[14] Stand therefore, having girded your waist with truth, having put on the breastplate of righteousness, [15] and having shod your feet with the preparation of the gospel of peace; [16] above all, taking the shield of faith with which you will be able to quench all the fiery darts of the wicked one. [17] And take the helmet of salvation, and the sword of the Spirit, which is the word of God; [18] praying always with all prayer and supplication in the Spirit, being watchful to this end with all perseverance and supplication for all the saints— [19] and for me, that utterance may be given to me, that I may open my mouth boldly to make known the mystery of the gospel, [20] for which I am an ambassador in chains; that in it I may speak boldly, as I ought to speak.

My thoughts about this scripture

_____
_____
_____
_____
_____
_____
_____
_____
_____
_____
_____
_____
_____

Day 257

Philippians 1 (New King James Version)

15 Some indeed preach Christ even from envy and strife, and some also from goodwill: 16 The former[b] preach Christ from selfish ambition, not sincerely, supposing to add affliction to my chains; 17 but the latter out of love, knowing that I am appointed for the defense of the gospel. 18 What then? Only that in every way, whether in pretense or in truth, Christ is preached; and in this I rejoice, yes, and will rejoice.

My thoughts about this scripture

_____
_____
_____
_____
_____
_____

When you talk to people about Christ are you sincere?

_____
_____

When you set someone on the right path, which is the path toward Christ, will they see you walking on that same path?

_____
_____
_____
_____
_____
_____
_____

Day 258

Isaiah 44 (New King James Version)

⁹ Those who make an image, all of them are useless,
And their precious things shall not profit;
They are their own witnesses;
They neither see nor know, that they may be ashamed.
¹⁰ Who would form a god or mold an image
That profits him nothing?
¹¹ Surely all his companions would be ashamed;
And the workmen, they are mere men.
Let them all be gathered together,
Let them stand up;
Yet they shall fear,
They shall be ashamed together.

Do you believe that if money is the most important thing in your life and you are willing to do anything, including defying God to get money, that you have made money a god?

_____

_____

_____

_____

_____

_____

My thoughts about this scripture

_____

_____

_____

_____

_____

_____

_____

_____

Day 259

Genesis 35 (New King James Version)

¹¹ Also God said to him: "I am God Almighty. Be fruitful and multiply; a nation and a company of nations shall proceed from you, and kings shall come from your body. ¹² The land which I gave Abraham and Isaac I give to you; and to your descendants after you I give this land." ¹³ Then God went up from him in the place where He talked with him. ¹⁴ So Jacob set up a pillar in the place where He talked with him, a pillar of stone; and he poured a drink offering on it, and he poured oil on it. ¹⁵ And Jacob called the name of the place where God spoke with him, Bethel.

Do you have a "Bethel", a place where you talk to God?

_____

_____

_____

_____

_____

_____

My thoughts about this scripture

_____

_____

_____

_____

_____

_____

_____

_____

Do you believe that God has said these same things to you?

_____

_____

_____

_____

_____

Nehemiah 13 (New King James Version)

14 Remember me, O my God, concerning this, and do not wipe out my good deeds that I have done for the house of my God, and for its services!

Make two lists below. One list is a list of things you did today that you are proud of and second will consist of things you are not so proud of. Once you've finished your "honest list of items", compare the two and see if "wiped out your good deeds".

Good List   *Not so good list*

Day 261

2 Chronicles 33 (New King James Version)

*[10] And the LORD spoke to Manasseh and his people, but they would not listen.
[11] Therefore the LORD brought upon them the captains of the army of the king of Assyria, who took Manasseh with hooks,[b] bound him with bronze fetters, and carried him off to Babylon. [12] Now when he was in affliction, he implored the LORD his God, and humbled himself greatly before the God of his fathers, [13] and prayed to Him; and He received his entreaty, heard his supplication, and brought him back to Jerusalem into his kingdom. Then Manasseh knew that the LORD was God.*

Write about a time when God had to remind you that He is LORD.

_____
_____
_____
_____
_____
_____
_____
_____
_____
_____
_____

Has that experience prevented you from making the same mistake again?

_____
_____
_____
_____
_____
_____

Day 262

Review

1. How many books are there in the Bible? _____
2. How many verses are there in Psalms? _____
3. Who was Ruth? _____
4. What were "The Twelve"? _____
5. The Bible is divided in the _____ testament and the ___ testament.
6. In what city was Jesus born? _____
7. How many wise men were there? _____
8. Why did Moses flee to Midian? _____
9. Who was Solomon's father? _____
10. How many plagues did Pharaoh suffer in Exodus? _____

Write a scripture from John (other than John 3:16)

_____
_____
_____
_____

Create three questions from the scripture you chose

1. _____

2. _____

3. _____

Ask your questions to a friend or family member to see how well they know John

Day 263

Deuteronomy 14 (Today's New International Version)

22 Be sure to set aside a tenth of all that your fields produce each year. 23 Eat the tithe of your grain, new wine and olive oil, and the firstborn of your herds and flocks in the presence of the LORD your God at the place he will choose as a dwelling for his Name, so that you may learn to revere the LORD your God always. 24 But if that place is too distant and you have been blessed by the LORD your God and cannot carry your tithe (because the place where the LORD will choose to put his Name is so far away), 25 then exchange your tithe for silver, and take the silver with you and go to the place the LORD your God will choose. 26 Use the silver to buy whatever you like: cattle, sheep, wine or other fermented drink, or anything you wish. Then you and your household shall eat there in the presence of the LORD your God and rejoice. 27 And do not neglect the Levites living in your towns, for they have no allotment or inheritance of their own.

28 At the end of every three years, bring all the tithes of that year's produce and store it in your towns, 29 so that the Levites (who have no allotment or inheritance of their own) and the foreigners, the fatherless and the widows who live in your towns may come and eat and be satisfied, and so that the LORD your God may bless you in all the work of your hands.

It is easy to stop reading this once you see grain and olive oil. You may feel that because you do not have flocks or herds you are not required to pay tithes. Please don't focus so much on what it is saying and miss what it means. If we have anything we are to give to those who have less. If we all do this, we will all have something.

May God continue to bless you so you may continue to bless others.

My thoughts about this scripture

_____
_____
_____
_____
_____
_____
_____
_____
_____

Day 264

Deuteronomy 29 (Today's New International Version)

¹ [a] These are the terms of the covenant the LORD commanded Moses to make with the Israelites in Moab, in addition to the covenant he had made with them at Horeb.

[b]2 Moses summoned all the Israelites and said to them:

Your eyes have seen all that the LORD did in Egypt to Pharaoh, to all his officials and to all his land. ³ With your own eyes you saw those great trials, those signs and great wonders. ⁴ But to this day the LORD has not given you a mind that understands or eyes that see or ears that hear. ⁵ During the forty years that I led you through the wilderness, your clothes did not wear out, nor did the sandals on your feet. ⁶ You ate no bread and drank no wine or other fermented drink. I did this so that you might know that I am the LORD your God.

⁷ When you reached this place, Sihon king of Heshbon and Og king of Bashan came out to fight against us, but we defeated them. ⁸ We took their land and gave it as an inheritance to the Reubenites, the Gadites and the half-tribe of Manasseh.

⁹ Carefully follow the terms of this covenant, so that you may prosper in everything you do.

My thoughts about this scripture

_____
_____
_____
_____
_____
_____
_____
_____

If God has provided for you during your travels, will you follow the terms of the covenant?

_____
_____
_____

Day 265

Exodus 5 (Today's New International Version)

15 Then the Israelite overseers went and appealed to Pharaoh: "Why have you treated your servants this way? 16 Your servants are given no straw, yet we are told, 'Make bricks!' Your servants are being beaten, but the fault is with your own people."

17 Pharaoh said, "Lazy, that's what you are—lazy! That is why you keep saying, 'Let us go and sacrifice to the LORD.' 18 Now get to work. You will not be given any straw, yet you must produce your full quota of bricks."

19 The Israelite overseers realized they were in trouble when they were told, "You are not to reduce the number of bricks required of you for each day." 20 When they left Pharaoh, they found Moses and Aaron waiting to meet them, 21 and they said, "May the LORD look on you and judge you! You have made us obnoxious to Pharaoh and his officials and have put a sword in their hand to kill us."

My thoughts about this scripture

_____
_____
_____
_____
_____
_____

What or who in your life is preventing you from celebrating God?

_____
_____
_____

Why do you allow it to happen?

_____
_____
_____

Day 266

Luke 15 (Today's New International Version)

¹ Now the tax collectors and sinners were all gathering around to hear Jesus. ² But the Pharisees and the teachers of the law muttered, "This man welcomes sinners and eats with them."

³ Then Jesus told them this parable: ⁴ "Suppose one of you has a hundred sheep and loses one of them. Doesn't he leave the ninety-nine in the open country and go after the lost sheep until he finds it? ⁵ And when he finds it, he joyfully puts it on his shoulders ⁶ and goes home. Then he calls his friends and neighbors together and says, 'Rejoice with me; I have found my lost sheep.' ⁷ I tell you that in the same way there will be more rejoicing in heaven over one sinner who repents than over ninety-nine righteous persons who do not need to repent.

My thoughts about this scripture

_____
_____
_____
_____
_____
_____
_____

Have you become "too saved" for your old friends who are not saved?

_____
_____
_____
_____
_____
_____

Day 267

Luke 16 (Today's New International Version)

8 "The master commended the dishonest manager because he had acted shrewdly. For the people of this world are more shrewd in dealing with their own kind than are the people of the light. 9 I tell you, use worldly wealth to gain friends for yourselves, so that when it is gone, you will be welcomed into eternal dwellings.

10 "Whoever can be trusted with very little can also be trusted with much, and whoever is dishonest with very little will also be dishonest with much. 11 So if you have not been trustworthy in handling worldly wealth, who will trust you with true riches? 12 And if you have not been trustworthy with someone else's property, who will give you property of your own?

13 "No one can serve two masters. Either you will hate the one and love the other, or you will be devoted to the one and despise the other. You cannot serve both God and money."

My thoughts about this scripture

_____
_____
_____
_____
_____
_____
_____

Are you honest with what you have? A better question is did you obtain what you have in an honest manner?

_____
_____
_____
_____
_____
_____

Day 268

Psalm 91 (Today's New International Version)

¹ Whoever dwells in the shelter of the Most High
will rest in the shadow of the Almighty.[a]
² They say of the LORD, "He is my refuge and my fortress,
my God, in whom I trust."

³ Surely he will save you
from the fowler's snare
and from the deadly pestilence.
⁴ He will cover you with his feathers,
and under his wings you will find refuge;
his faithfulness will be your shield and rampart.
⁵ You will not fear the terror of night,
nor the arrow that flies by day,
⁶ nor the pestilence that stalks in the darkness,
nor the plague that destroys at midday.
⁷ A thousand may fall at your side,
ten thousand at your right hand,
but it will not come near you.
⁸ You will only observe with your eyes
and see the punishment of the wicked.

My thoughts about this scripture

_____
_____
_____
_____
_____
_____
_____
_____
_____

Be blessed in the LORD this day, for this day is surely a blessing from our LORD.

Day 269

Psalm 140 (Today's New International Version)

[1] Rescue me, LORD, from evildoers;
protect me from the violent,
[2] who devise evil plans in their hearts
and stir up war every day.
[3] They make their tongues as sharp as a serpent's;
the poison of vipers is on their lips.[b]

[4] Keep me safe, LORD, from the hands of the wicked;
protect me from the violent,
who devise ways to trip my feet.
[5] The arrogant have hidden a snare for me;
they have spread out the cords of their net
and have set traps for me along my path.

[6] I say to the LORD, "You are my God."
Hear, LORD, my cry for mercy.
[7] Sovereign LORD, my strong deliverer,
you shield my head in the day of battle.
[8] Do not grant the wicked their desires, LORD;
do not let their plans succeed.

My thoughts about this scripture

_____
_____
_____
_____
_____
_____
_____
_____
_____
_____
_____
_____
_____
_____
_____

Day 270

Genesis 2 (Today's New International Version)

4 This is the account of the heavens and the earth when they were created, when the LORD God made the earth and the heavens.

5 Now no shrub had yet appeared on the earth[a] and no plant had yet sprung up, for the LORD God had not sent rain on the earth and there was no one to work the ground, 6 but streams[b] came up from the earth and watered the whole surface of the ground. 7 Then the LORD God formed a man[c] from the dust of the ground and breathed into his nostrils the breath of life, and the man became a living being.

My thoughts about this scripture

_____
_____
_____
_____
_____
_____
_____
_____
_____
_____

Day 271

James 1 (New International Version)

⁹ Believers in humble circumstances ought to take pride in their high position. ¹⁰ But the rich should take pride in their humiliation—since they will pass away like a wild flower. ¹¹ For the sun rises with scorching heat and withers the plant; its blossom falls and its beauty is destroyed. In the same way, the rich will fade away even while they go about their business.

¹² Blessed is the one who perseveres under trial because, having stood the test, that person will receive the crown of life that the Lord has promised to those who love him.

¹³ When tempted, no one should say, "God is tempting me." For God cannot be tempted by evil, nor does he tempt anyone; ¹⁴ but each person is tempted when they are dragged away by their own evil desire and enticed. ¹⁵ Then, after desire has conceived, it gives birth to sin; and sin, when it is full-grown, gives birth to death.

¹⁶ Don't be deceived, my dear brothers and sisters. ¹⁷ Every good and perfect gift is from above, coming down from the Father of the heavenly lights, who does not change like shifting shadows. ¹⁸ He chose to give us birth through the word of truth, that we might be a kind of firstfruits of all he created.

My thoughts about this scripture

_____

_____

_____

_____

_____

_____

_____

_____

_____

_____

Day 272

James 3 (New International Version)

¹ Not many of you should become teachers, my fellow believers, because you know that we who teach will be judged more strictly. ² We all stumble in many ways. Anyone who is never at fault in what they say is perfect, able to keep their whole body in check.

³ When we put bits into the mouths of horses to make them obey us, we can turn the whole animal. ⁴ Or take ships as an example. Although they are so large and are driven by strong winds, they are steered by a very small rudder wherever the pilot wants to go. ⁵ Likewise, the tongue is a small part of the body, but it makes great boasts. Consider what a great forest is set on fire by a small spark. ⁶ The tongue also is a fire, a world of evil among the parts of the body. It corrupts the whole body, sets the whole course of one's life on fire, and is itself set on fire by hell.

My thoughts about this scripture

_____
_____
_____
_____
_____
_____

Are you careful about what you say or do you feel it is more important to make your point?

_____
_____
_____
_____
_____

Do you believe that a "small spark" or saying something simple could cause a great fire in someone's life?

_____
_____
_____

Day 273

Psalm 46 (New King James Version)

⁴ There is a river whose streams shall make glad the city of God,
The holy place of the tabernacle of the Most High.
⁵ God is in the midst of her, she shall not be moved;
God shall help her, just at the break of dawn.
⁶ The nations raged, the kingdoms were moved;
He uttered His voice, the earth melted.

⁷ The LORD of hosts is with us;
The God of Jacob is our refuge.

My thoughts about this scripture

_____
_____
_____
_____
_____
_____
_____
_____
_____
_____

Day 274

Romans 6 (New King James Version)

¹⁵ What then? Shall we sin because we are not under law but under grace? Certainly not! ¹⁶ Do you not know that to whom you present yourselves slaves to obey, you are that one's slaves whom you obey, whether of sin leading to death, or of obedience leading to righteousness? ¹⁷ But God be thanked that though you were slaves of sin, yet you obeyed from the heart that form of doctrine to which you were delivered. ¹⁸ And having been set free from sin, you became slaves of righteousness. ¹⁹ I speak in human terms because of the weakness of your flesh. For just as you presented your members as slaves of uncleanness, and of lawlessness leading to more lawlessness, so now present your members as slaves of righteousness for holiness.

²⁰ For when you were slaves of sin, you were free in regard to righteousness. ²¹ What fruit did you have then in the things of which you are now ashamed? For the end of those things is death. ²² But now having been set free from sin, and having become slaves of God, you have your fruit to holiness, and the end, everlasting life. ²³ For the wages of sin is death, but the gift of God is eternal life in Christ Jesus our Lord.

My thoughts about this scripture

_____

_____

_____

_____

_____

_____

_____

Why will people stand up and clap at a concert but will not stand up and praise God who has given them the gift of eternal life?

_____

_____

_____

_____

_____

_____

Day 275

Amos 4 (New King James Version)

Hear this word, you cows of Bashan, who are on the mountain of Samaria,
Who oppress the poor,
Who crush the needy,
Who say to your husbands,[a] "Bring wine, let us drink!"
2 The Lord GOD has sworn by His holiness:
"Behold, the days shall come upon you
When He will take you away with fishhooks,
And your posterity with fishhooks.
3 You will go out through broken walls,
Each one straight ahead of her,
And you will be cast into Harmon,"
Says the LORD.

My thoughts about this scripture

_____
_____
_____
_____
_____
_____
_____

How charitable are you? (Not just with your money but with time, love and compassion)

_____
_____
_____
_____
_____

Day 276

Proverbs 15 (New King James Version)

A soft answer turns away wrath,
But a harsh word stirs up anger.
² The tongue of the wise uses knowledge rightly,
But the mouth of fools pours forth foolishness.

³ The eyes of the LORD are in every place,
Keeping watch on the evil and the good.

⁴ A wholesome tongue is a tree of life,
But perverseness in it breaks the spirit.

⁵ A fool despises his father's instruction,
But he who receives correction is prudent.

⁶ In the house of the righteous there is much treasure,
But in the revenue of the wicked is trouble.

⁷ The lips of the wise disperse knowledge,
But the heart of the fool does not do so.

⁸ The sacrifice of the wicked is an abomination to the LORD,
But the prayer of the upright is His delight.
⁹ The way of the wicked is an abomination to the LORD,
But He loves him who follows righteousness.

¹⁰ Harsh discipline is for him who forsakes the way,
And he who hates correction will die.

¹¹ Hell[a] and Destruction[b] are before the LORD;
So how much more the hearts of the sons of men.

¹² A scoffer does not love one who corrects him,
Nor will he go to the wise.

¹³ A merry heart makes a cheerful countenance,
But by sorrow of the heart the spirit is broken.

¹⁴ The heart of him who has understanding seeks knowledge,
But the mouth of fools feeds on foolishness

Day 277

Isaiah 28 (New King James Version)

²³ Give ear and hear my voice,
Listen and hear my speech.
²⁴ Does the plowman keep plowing all day to sow?
Does he keep turning his soil and breaking the clods?
²⁵ When he has leveled its surface,
Does he not sow the black cummin
And scatter the cummin,
Plant the wheat in rows,
The barley in the appointed place,
And the spelt in its place?
²⁶ For He instructs him in right judgment,
His God teaches him.
²⁷ For the black cummin is not threshed with a threshing sledge,
Nor is a cartwheel rolled over the cummin;
But the black cummin is beaten out with a stick,
And the cummin with a rod.
²⁸ Bread flour must be ground;
Therefore he does not thresh it forever,
Break it with his cartwheel,
Or crush it with his horsemen.
²⁹ This also comes from the LORD of hosts,
Who is wonderful in counsel and excellent in guidance.

My thoughts about this scripture

_____
_____
_____
_____
_____
_____
_____
_____
_____

Day 278

Positive Points

Find words and write them below

```
J  G  B  C  W  I  G  E  W  I  S  C  C  Y  M
E  C  N  D  L  N  A  X  U  Z  W  Z  W  J  L
G  N  P  E  I  A  T  G  G  H  P  U  J  S  F
N  L  P  V  T  E  I  R  K  N  K  L  J  O  I
I  S  I  R  E  M  M  B  P  N  I  I  G  Y  H
R  G  Z  S  A  L  E  U  G  Q  E  G  C  Q  G
I  Z  W  A  C  I  G  P  A  T  I  E  N  C  E
P  H  Q  S  H  N  S  Z  W  W  P  G  Z  I  Z
S  X  Y  A  I  F  R  I  O  Q  J  N  F  P  S
N  B  J  T  N  L  M  R  N  X  R  I  E  P  A
I  J  F  J  G  O  S  L  R  G  Z  R  D  O  E
E  I  J  L  O  H  R  G  N  I  R  A  H  S  H
L  O  V  E  I  Y  R  E  Z  F  J  C  Q  B  X
G  R  H  P  L  B  Y  M  C  P  I  U  Z  P  N
Y  N  H  W  V  Q  B  I  D  R  G  A  N  G  I
```

_____   _____   _____

_____   ___ ___   _____

_____   _____   _____

_____   _____   _____

Day 279

Genesis 13 (New King James Version)

⁵ Lot also, who went with Abram, had flocks and herds and tents. ⁶ Now the land was not able to support them, that they might dwell together, for their possessions were so great that they could not dwell together. ⁷ And there was strife between the herdsmen of Abram's livestock and the herdsmen of Lot's livestock. The Canaanites and the Perizzites then dwelt in the land.

⁸ So Abram said to Lot, "Please let there be no strife between you and me, and between my herdsmen and your herdsmen; for we are brethren. ⁹ Is not the whole land before you? Please separate from me. If you take the left, then I will go to the right; or, if you go to the right, then I will go to the left."

¹⁰ And Lot lifted his eyes and saw all the plain of Jordan, that it was well watered everywhere (before the LORD destroyed Sodom and Gomorrah) like the garden of the LORD, like the land of Egypt as you go toward Zoar. ¹¹ Then Lot chose for himself all the plain of Jordan, and Lot journeyed east. And they separated from each other. ¹² Abram dwelt in the land of Canaan, and Lot dwelt in the cities of the plain and pitched his tent even as far as Sodom. ¹³ But the men of Sodom were exceedingly wicked and sinful against the LORD.

¹⁴ And the LORD said to Abram, after Lot had separated from him: "Lift your eyes now and look from the place where you are—northward, southward, eastward, and westward; ¹⁵ for all the land which you see I give to you and your descendants[b] forever. ¹⁶ And I will make your descendants as the dust of the earth; so that if a man could number the dust of the earth, then your descendants also could be numbered. ¹⁷ Arise, walk in the land through its length and its width, for I give it to you."

¹⁸ Then Abram moved his tent, and went and dwelt by the terebinth trees of Mamre,[c] which are in Hebron, and built an altar there to the LORD.

In Abram's attempt to settle things in a Godly manner, to not fight over what was the best or the largest he was blessed. Will you settle for less with man so you can have more with God?

_____

_____

_____

_____

Day 280

"Bride without a Budget"

Wanda was a blushing bride and was the type to spare no expenses for her wedding. She ordered flowers from Paris, the China from Spain the food from Italy and it would all be arranged by Igor, the most expensive,…. I mean most well know, wedding planner in New York.

Wanda's soon to be husband was a professional Basketball player, her father a successful Attorney and her mother was a professor at a local college. Wanda was, well she was related to them. Who made the money wasn't important to Wanda, only what it was used to purchase mattered to her.

After everything was perfect, according to Wanda and Igor of course, she handed her father a bill of over $150,000 dollars for the wedding. Both her parents tried to reason with her but she refused to listen, repeating it was her day and it should be as she wanted it.

Matthew, the groom, found Wanda in the kitchen where he tried to reason with her. Again, she would not listen. Finally Matthew asked if she was like this now, would she be worse once they were married. He pointed out that they were both getting married and he should have some input about it. Wanda disagreed and stated if she couldn't have the wedding her way then she just wouldn't get married at all.

Matthew said he understood, kissed her on the forehead and walked out of the kitchen. Wanda, being so selfish and only thinking of herself, assumed Matthew was going to tell her parents what she said and her wedding would be the way she always dreamt it would be. However, a couple hours passed and Matthew had not returned to the kitchen.

When Wanda walked into the backyard, she saw her parents sitting in the gazebo drinking wine and laughing. Wanda immediately ran over to them and asked what happened, where was Matthew? Her father explained that Matthew told them about the conversation that he had with her and was sorry that there wouldn't be a wedding. Wanda could not believe her ears, she couldn't understand why Matthew left and since he left, why were they drinking wine and laughing.

Her mother explained to her that because of her self-centeredness, they understood Matthew's fear. She explained further that they were all concerned that Wanda's first love was money and then herself and then money again. And that if she wanted him back, she need to learn to love some other than herself.

Is Wanda's issue her own fault, the fault of her parents or her fiancé?

_____

_____

_____

_____

Is a selfish love a Godless love? Explain.

_____

_____

_____

_____

Psalm 49 (New King James Version)

10 For he sees wise men die;
Likewise the fool and the senseless person perish,
And leave their wealth to others.
11 Their inner thought is that their houses will last forever,[a]
Their dwelling places to all generations;
They call their lands after their own names.
12 Nevertheless man, though in honor, does not remain;[b]
He is like the beasts that perish.

13 This is the way of those who are foolish,

In your pursuit of wealth and power, do you ever consider who is next in line?

_____

Do you consider if your children share the same desires you have?

_____

So, if you spend your life trying to accumulate things and your children don't like clutter, what have you accomplished?

_____
_____

Is it not wiser to spend your time pursuing the Lord so you can enjoy the treasures He has accumulated for you?

_____
_____
_____
_____

Day 282

1 Samuel 2 (New King James Version)

And Hannah prayed and said:

"My heart rejoices in the LORD;
My horn[a] is exalted in the LORD.
I smile at my enemies,
Because I rejoice in Your salvation.

2 "No one is holy like the LORD,
For there is none besides You,
Nor is there any rock like our God.

3 "Talk no more so very proudly;
Let no arrogance come from your mouth,
For the LORD is the God of knowledge;
And by Him actions are weighed.

4 "The bows of the mighty men are broken,
And those who stumbled are girded with strength.
5 Those who were full have hired themselves out for bread,
And the hungry have ceased to hunger.
Even the barren has borne seven,
And she who has many children has become feeble.

6 "The LORD kills and makes alive;
He brings down to the grave and brings up.
7 The LORD makes poor and makes rich;
He brings low and lifts up.
8 He raises the poor from the dust
And lifts the beggar from the ash heap,
To set them among princes
And make them inherit the throne of glory.

"For the pillars of the earth are the LORD's,
And He has set the world upon them.
9 He will guard the feet of His saints,
But the wicked shall be silent in darkness.
"For by strength no man shall prevail.
10 The adversaries of the LORD shall be broken in pieces;
From heaven He will thunder against them.
The LORD will judge the ends of the earth.

Day 283

2 Samuel 11 (New King James Version)

² Then it happened one evening that David arose from his bed and walked on the roof of the king's house. And from the roof he saw a woman bathing, and the woman was very beautiful to behold. ³ So David sent and inquired about the woman. And someone said, "Is this not Bathsheba, the daughter of Eliam, the wife of Uriah the Hittite?" ⁴ Then David sent messengers, and took her; and she came to him, and he lay with her, for she was cleansed from her impurity; and she returned to her house. ⁵ And the woman conceived; so she sent and told David, and said, "I am with child."

My thoughts about this scripture

_____

_____

_____

_____

_____

_____

Other than taking another man's wife, write something else David did that would not be approved by God?

_____

_____

_____

_____

_____

Day 284

2 Chronicles 1 (New King James Version)

⁷ On that night God appeared to Solomon, and said to him, "Ask! What shall I give you?"

⁸ And Solomon said to God: "You have shown great mercy to David my father, and have made me king in his place. ⁹ Now, O LORD God, let Your promise to David my father be established, for You have made me king over a people like the dust of the earth in multitude. ¹⁰ Now give me wisdom and knowledge, that I may go out and come in before this people; for who can judge this great people of Yours?"

¹¹ Then God said to Solomon: "Because this was in your heart, and you have not asked riches or wealth or honor or the life of your enemies, nor have you asked long life— but have asked wisdom and knowledge for yourself, that you may judge My people over whom I have made you king— ¹² wisdom and knowledge are granted to you; and I will give you riches and wealth and honor, such as none of the kings have had who were before you, nor shall any after you have the like."

My thoughts about this scripture

_____
_____
_____
_____
_____
_____
_____

What would you ask God for?

_____
_____
_____
_____
_____

Day 285

Do not envy anyone for God has plans for you. What they have may work for them but it may not work for you.

<u>Job 5:2</u>
For wrath kills a foolish man, And **envy** slays a simple one.

<u>Psalm 68:16</u>
Why do you fume with **envy**, you mountains of many peaks? This is the mountain which God desires to dwell in; Yes, the LORD will dwell in it forever.

<u>Proverbs 3:31</u>
Do not **envy** the oppressor, And choose none of his ways;

<u>Acts 13:45</u>
But when the Jews saw the multitudes, they were filled with **envy**; and contradicting and blaspheming, they opposed the things spoken by Paul.

<u>Galatians 5:26</u>
Let us not become conceited, provoking one another, **envy**ing one another.

<u>1 Timothy 6:4</u>
he is proud, knowing nothing, but is obsessed with disputes and arguments over words, from which come **envy**, strife, reviling, evil suspicions,

<u>James 3:16</u>
For where **envy** and self-seeking exist, confusion and every evil thing are there.

<u>1 Corinthians 13:4</u>
Love suffers long and is kind; love does not **envy**; love does not parade itself, is not puffed up;

Day 286

Titus 3 (New King James Version)

[8] This is a faithful saying, and these things I want you to affirm constantly, that those who have believed in God should be careful to maintain good works. These things are good and profitable to men.

[9] But avoid foolish disputes, genealogies, contentions, and strivings about the law; for they are unprofitable and useless. [10] Reject a divisive man after the first and second admonition, [11] knowing that such a person is warped and sinning, being self-condemned.

My thoughts about this scripture

_____
_____
_____
_____
_____
_____
_____

How much time have you wasted disputing things that do not matter?

_____
_____

How many times have you allowed the enemy to use you to start that dispute?

_____
_____

Now that you know the trick of the devil, how will you handle disputes or disagreements in the future?

_____
_____
_____
_____
_____
_____

Day 287

Acts 26 (New King James Version)

⁹ "Indeed, I myself thought I must do many things contrary to the name of Jesus of Nazareth. ¹⁰ This I also did in Jerusalem, and many of the saints I shut up in prison, having received authority from the chief priests; and when they were put to death, I cast my vote against them. ¹¹ And I punished them often in every synagogue and compelled them to blaspheme; and being exceedingly enraged against them, I persecuted them even to foreign cities.

¹² "While thus occupied, as I journeyed to Damascus with authority and commission from the chief priests, ¹³ at midday, O king, along the road I saw a light from heaven, brighter than the sun, shining around me and those who journeyed with me. ¹⁴ And when we all had fallen to the ground, I heard a voice speaking to me and saying in the Hebrew language, 'Saul, Saul, why are you persecuting Me? It is hard for you to kick against the goads.' ¹⁵ So I said, 'Who are You, Lord?' And He said, 'I am Jesus, whom you are persecuting. ¹⁶ But rise and stand on your feet; for I have appeared to you for this purpose, to make you a minister and a witness both of the things which you have seen and of the things which I will yet reveal to you. ¹⁷ I will deliver you from the Jewish people, as well as from the Gentiles, to whom I now[a] send you, ¹⁸ to open their eyes, in order to turn them from darkness to light, and from the power of Satan to God, that they may receive forgiveness of sins and an inheritance among those who are sanctified by faith in Me.'

My thoughts about this scripture

_____
_____
_____
_____
_____
_____

Do you persecute Christians?

_____

Really? Have you spoken negatively about a Christian or a church that may have turned away a soul that wanted to be saved?

_____
_____
_____
_____

Day 288

Amos 5 (New King James Version)

¹⁴ Seek good and not evil,
That you may live;
So the LORD God of hosts will be with you,
As you have spoken.
¹⁵ Hate evil, love good;
Establish justice in the gate.
It may be that the LORD God of hosts
Will be gracious to the remnant of Joseph

¹⁸ Woe to you who desire the day of the LORD!
For what good is the day of the LORD to you?
It will be darkness, and not light.
¹⁹ It will be as though a man fled from a lion,
And a bear met him!
Or as though he went into the house,
Leaned his hand on the wall,
And a serpent bit him!
²⁰ Is not the day of the LORD darkness, and not light?
Is it not very dark, with no brightness in it?

My thoughts about this scripture

_____
_____
_____
_____
_____
_____
_____
_____

Day 289

Genesis 25 (New King James Version)

⁷ This is the sum of the years of Abraham's life which he lived: one hundred and seventy-five years. ⁸ Then Abraham breathed his last and died in a good old age, an old man and full of years, and was gathered to his people. ⁹ And his sons Isaac and Ishmael buried him in the cave of Machpelah, which is before Mamre, in the field of Ephron the son of Zohar the Hittite, ¹⁰ the field which Abraham purchased from the sons of Heth. There Abraham was buried, and Sarah his wife. ¹¹ And it came to pass, after the death of Abraham, that God blessed his son Isaac. And Isaac dwelt at Beer Lahai Roi.

My thoughts about this scripture

_____
_____
_____
_____
_____
_____

Name one of Abraham's sons. _____

How old was Abraham when he died? _____

What was his wife's name? _____

What was the name of his final resting place? _____

Day 290

Matthew 25 (New King James Version)

"Then the kingdom of heaven shall be likened to ten virgins who took their lamps and went out to meet the bridegroom. [2] Now five of them were wise, and five were foolish. [3] Those who were foolish took their lamps and took no oil with them, [4] but the wise took oil in their vessels with their lamps. [5] But while the bridegroom was delayed, they all slumbered and slept.

[6] "And at midnight a cry was heard: 'Behold, the bridegroom is coming;[a] go out to meet him!' [7] Then all those virgins arose and trimmed their lamps. [8] And the foolish said to the wise, 'Give us some of your oil, for our lamps are going out.' [9] But the wise answered, saying, 'No, lest there should not be enough for us and you; but go rather to those who sell, and buy for yourselves.' [10] And while they went to buy, the bridegroom came, and those who were ready went in with him to the wedding; and the door was shut.

[11] "Afterward the other virgins came also, saying, 'Lord, Lord, open to us!' [12] But he answered and said, 'Assuredly, I say to you, I do not know you.'

[13] "Watch therefore, for you know neither the day nor the hour[b] in which the Son of Man is coming.

My thoughts about this scripture

_____
_____
_____
_____
_____
_____

Being prepared and being ready could be the main purpose of this parable? Do you agree? Explain.

_____
_____
_____
_____
_____
_____

Day 291

Genesis 45 (New King James Version)

⁹ "Hurry and go up to my father, and say to him, 'Thus says your son Joseph: "God has made me lord of all Egypt; come down to me, do not tarry. ¹⁰ You shall dwell in the land of Goshen, and you shall be near to me, you and your children, your children's children, your flocks and your herds, and all that you have. ¹¹ There I will provide for you, lest you and your household, and all that you have, come to poverty; for there are still five years of famine."'

My thoughts about this scripture

_____
_____
_____
_____
_____

²⁵ Then they went up out of Egypt, and came to the land of Canaan to Jacob their father. ²⁶ And they told him, saying, "Joseph is still alive, and he is governor over all the land of Egypt." And Jacob's heart stood still, because he did not believe them. ²⁷ But when they told him all the words which Joseph had said to them, and when he saw the carts which Joseph had sent to carry him, the spirit of Jacob their father revived. ²⁸ Then Israel said, "It is enough. Joseph my son is still alive. I will go and see him before I die."

My thoughts about this scripture

_____
_____
_____
_____
_____
_____
_____
_____
_____

Day 292

Deuteronomy 11 (New King James Version)

[13] 'And it shall be that if you earnestly obey My commandments which I command you today, to love the LORD your God and serve Him with all your heart and with all your soul, [14] then I[b] will give you the rain for your land in its season, the early rain and the latter rain, that you may gather in your grain, your new wine, and your oil. [15] And I will send grass in your fields for your livestock, that you may eat and be filled.' [16] "Take heed to yourselves, lest your heart be deceived, and you turn aside and serve other gods and worship them, [17] lest the LORD's anger be aroused against you, and He shut up the heavens so that there be no rain, and the land yield no produce, and you perish quickly from the good land which the LORD is giving you.

[18] "Therefore you shall lay up these words of mine in your heart and in your soul, and bind them as a sign on your hand, and they shall be as frontlets between your eyes. [19] You shall teach them to your children, speaking of them when you sit in your house, when you walk by the way, when you lie down, and when you rise up. [20] And you shall write them on the doorposts of your house and on your gates, [21] that your days and the days of your children may be multiplied in the land of which the LORD swore to your fathers to give them, like the days of the heavens above the earth.

My thoughts about this scripture

_____
_____
_____
_____
_____

Do you store up God's words in your heart so you can provide them whenever someone else needs them?

_____
_____
_____
_____
_____
_____
_____

Day 293

Exodus 33 (New King James Version)

17 So the LORD said to Moses, "I will also do this thing that you have spoken; for you have found grace in My sight, and I know you by name."

18 And he said, "Please, show me Your glory."

19 Then He said, "I will make all My goodness pass before you, and I will proclaim the name of the LORD before you. I will be gracious to whom I will be gracious, and I will have compassion on whom I will have compassion." 20 But He said, "You cannot see My face; for no man shall see Me, and live." 21 And the LORD said, "Here is a place by Me, and you shall stand on the rock. 22 So it shall be, while My glory passes by, that I will put you in the cleft of the rock, and will cover you with My hand while I pass by. 23 Then I will take away My hand, and you shall see My back; but My face shall not be seen."

My thoughts about this scripture

_____
_____
_____
_____
_____
_____
_____

Write about a time God showed you His glory

_____
_____
_____
_____
_____
_____

Day 294

Write about a recent event that has happened to you (good or bad). As you write mention how the event affected you that day and explain how your reaction would have been different had God not given you His Holy Spirit to guide you.

_____
_____
_____
_____
_____
_____
_____
_____
_____
_____
_____
_____
_____
_____

What other differences do you see in your personality since you've allowed God to lead you?

_____
_____
_____
_____
_____
_____
_____
_____
_____
_____
_____
_____

Day 295

Ezra 6 (New King James Version)

3 In the first year of King Cyrus, King Cyrus issued a decree concerning the house of God at Jerusalem: "Let the house be rebuilt, the place where they offered sacrifices; and let the foundations of it be firmly laid, its height sixty cubits and its width sixty cubits, 4 with three rows of heavy stones and one row of new timber. Let the expenses be paid from the king's treasury. 5 Also let the gold and silver articles of the house of God, which Nebuchadnezzar took from the temple which is in Jerusalem and brought to Babylon, be restored and taken back to the temple which is in Jerusalem, each to its place; and deposit them in the house of God"—

My thoughts about this scripture

_____
_____
_____
_____
_____
_____

When we think of "House of God", we think of a church but do you consider your home a house of God?

_____
_____

If yes, what are you doing to rebuild God's house as it was?

_____
_____
_____
_____
_____
_____

If no,……..well let's just hope everyone said yes.

Have a blessed day in your House of God

Day 296

1 Chronicles 22 (New King James Version)

⁶ Then he called for his son Solomon, and charged him to build a house for the LORD God of Israel. ⁷ And David said to Solomon: "My son, as for me, it was in my mind to build a house to the name of the LORD my God; ⁸ but the word of the LORD came to me, saying, 'You have shed much blood and have made great wars; you shall not build a house for My name, because you have shed much blood on the earth in My sight. ⁹ Behold, a son shall be born to you, who shall be a man of rest; and I will give him rest from all his enemies all around. His name shall be Solomon,[a] for I will give peace and quietness to Israel in his days. ¹⁰ He shall build a house for My name, and he shall be My son, and I will be his Father; and I will establish the throne of his kingdom over Israel forever.' ¹¹ Now, my son, may the LORD be with you; and may you prosper, and build the house of the LORD your God, as He has said to you.

One of your questions yesterday was if your home was a house of God. Hopefully you said yes, so today is "part two" for that question

Are your children a part of the construction in transforming your home into a house of God? Explain.

_____
_____
_____
_____
_____
_____
_____
_____
_____

Do your friends and extended family respect your efforts to transform your home into a house of God? Explain.

_____
_____
_____
_____
_____
_____
_____

the house of the LORD, was filled with a cloud, ¹⁴ so that the priests could not continue ministering because of the cloud; for the glory of the LORD filled the house of God.

Day 297

Genesis 27 (New King James Version)

Now it came to pass, when Isaac was old and his eyes were so dim that he could not see, that he called Esau his older son and said to him, "My son."

And he answered him, "Here I am."

² Then he said, "Behold now, I am old. I do not know the day of my death. ³ Now therefore, please take your weapons, your quiver and your bow, and go out to the field and hunt game for me. ⁴ And make me savory food, such as I love, and bring it to me that I may eat, that my soul may bless you before I die."

⁵ Now Rebekah was listening when Isaac spoke to Esau his son. And Esau went to the field to hunt game and to bring it. ⁶ So Rebekah spoke to Jacob her son, saying, "Indeed I heard your father speak to Esau your brother, saying, ⁷ 'Bring me game and make savory food for me, that I may eat it and bless you in the presence of the LORD before my death.' ⁸ Now therefore, my son, obey my voice according to what I command you. ⁹ Go now to the flock and bring me from there two choice kids of the goats, and I will make savory food from them for your father, such as he loves. ¹⁰ Then you shall take it to your father, that he may eat it, and that he may bless you before his death."

My thoughts about this scripture

_____
_____
_____
_____
_____
_____
_____

As parents, do we sometimes lead our children away from God and not towards Him?

_____
_____
_____
_____
_____
_____

Day 298

Deuteronomy 17 (New King James Version)

"You shall not sacrifice to the LORD your God a bull or sheep which has any blemish or defect, for that is an abomination to the LORD your God.

My thoughts about this scripture

_____
_____
_____
_____
_____
_____
_____
_____

In this scripture, what if you replaced "a bull or sheep" and use "your heart or a promise? And maybe replace "blemish or defect" with "deceit or unfaithfulness"?

_____
_____
_____
_____
_____
_____
_____
_____

Day 299

Mark 7 (New King James Version)

⁵ Then the Pharisees and scribes asked Him, "Why do Your disciples not walk according to the tradition of the elders, but eat bread with unwashed hands?"

⁶ He answered and said to them, "Well did Isaiah prophesy of you hypocrites, as it is written:

'This people honors Me with their lips,
But their heart is far from Me.
⁷ And in vain they worship Me,
Teaching as doctrines the commandments of men.'[b]

⁸ For laying aside the commandment of God, you hold the tradition of men[c] —the washing of pitchers and cups, and many other such things you do."

⁹ He said to them, "All too well you reject the commandment of God, that you may keep your tradition.

People get so wrapped up in what their family has done for years but tend not to do what God requires. Do you feel that people sometimes get tradition and religion confused?

_____
_____
_____
_____
_____
_____
_____
_____

My thoughts about this scripture

_____
_____
_____
_____
_____
_____
_____

Day 300

Review

1. Who did David enlist to build the house of God? _____
2. Who were the earthly parents of Jesus? _____ and _____
3. How many books are there in the Bible? _____
4. Who was Solomon's father? _____
5. What book follows Matthew? _____
6. What was Ruth's relationship with Naomi? _____
7. Name three disciples. _____, _____ and _____
8. In the beginning God created the _____ and the _____
9. _____ baptized Jesus with water.
10. _____ is associated with the lion's den.

Write in the following;

John 3:16

_____
_____
_____

Matthew 10:32-33

_____
_____
_____
_____
_____

Psalm 95:1-2

_____
_____
_____
_____
_____

Day 301

Deuteronomy 33 (New King James Version)

¹² Of Benjamin he said:

"The beloved of the LORD shall dwell in safety by Him,
Who shelters him all the day long;
And he shall dwell between His shoulders."

¹³ And of Joseph he said:

"Blessed of the LORD is his land,
With the precious things of heaven, with the dew,
And the deep lying beneath,
¹⁴ With the precious fruits of the sun,
With the precious produce of the months,
¹⁵ With the best things of the ancient mountains,
With the precious things of the everlasting hills,
¹⁶ With the precious things of the earth and its fullness,
And the favor of Him who dwelt in the bush.
Let the blessing come 'on the head of Joseph,
And on the crown of the head of him who was separate from his brothers." [a]*
¹⁷ His glory is like a firstborn bull,
And his horns like the horns of the wild ox;
Together with them
He shall push the peoples
To the ends of the earth;
They are the ten thousands of Ephraim,
And they are the thousands of Manasseh."

¹⁸ And of Zebulun he said:

"Rejoice, Zebulun, in your going out,
And Issachar in your tents!
¹⁹ They shall call the peoples to the mountain;
There they shall offer sacrifices of righteousness;
For they shall partake of the abundance of the seas
And of treasures hidden in the sand."

Day 302

Ecclesiastes 7 (New King James Version)

²⁰ For there is not a just man on earth who does good
And does not sin.

²¹ Also do not take to heart everything people say,
Lest you hear your servant cursing you.
²² For many times, also, your own heart has known
That even you have cursed others.

²³ All this I have proved by wisdom.
I said, "I will be wise";
But it was far from me.
²⁴ As for that which is far off and exceedingly deep,
Who can find it out?
²⁵ I applied my heart to know,
To search and seek out wisdom and the reason of things,
To know the wickedness of folly,
Even of foolishness and madness.
²⁶ And I find more bitter than death
The woman whose heart is snares and nets,
Whose hands are fetters.
He who pleases God shall escape from her,
But the sinner shall be trapped by her.

My thoughts about this scripture

_____
_____
_____
_____
_____
_____
_____
_____
_____

Day 303

TODAY FOCUS ON LOVING GOD

Write what you will do today to express your love for God

_____
_____
_____
_____
_____
_____
_____

Remember, it is impossible to love God and not love his children. Write how you will express your love for the people around you today.

_____
_____
_____
_____
_____
_____
_____

The Bible tells us that if we do not do for the least of us we have not done for Christ. Write what you will do this week to help someone in need.

_____
_____
_____
_____
_____
_____

Day 304

Deuteronomy 9 (New King James Version)

[7] "Remember! Do not forget how you provoked the LORD your God to wrath in the wilderness. From the day that you departed from the land of Egypt until you came to this place, you have been rebellious against the LORD. [8] Also in Horeb you provoked the LORD to wrath, so that the LORD was angry enough with you to have destroyed you. [9] When I went up into the mountain to receive the tablets of stone, the tablets of the covenant which the LORD made with you, then I stayed on the mountain forty days and forty nights. I neither ate bread nor drank water. [10] Then the LORD delivered to me two tablets of stone written with the finger of God, and on them were all the words which the LORD had spoken to you on the mountain from the midst of the fire in the day of the assembly. [11] And it came to pass, at the end of forty days and forty nights, that the LORD gave me the two tablets of stone, the tablets of the covenant.

[12] "Then the LORD said to me, 'Arise, go down quickly from here, for your people whom you brought out of Egypt have acted corruptly; they have quickly turned aside from the way which I commanded them; they have made themselves a molded image.'

My thoughts about this scripture

_____

_____

_____

_____

_____

_____

_____

_____

Do you know someone who is truly blessed but they don't seem to appreciate it?

_____

_____

_____

_____

_____

Day 305

2 Samuel 11 (New King James Version)

² Then it happened one evening that David arose from his bed and walked on the roof of the king's house. And from the roof he saw a woman bathing, and the woman was very beautiful to behold. ³ So David sent and inquired about the woman. And someone said, "Is this not Bathsheba, the daughter of Eliam, the wife of Uriah the Hittite?" ⁴ Then David sent messengers, and took her; and she came to him, and he lay with her, for she was cleansed from her impurity; and she returned to her house. ⁵ And the woman conceived; so she sent and told David, and said, "I am with child."

¹⁴ In the morning it happened that David wrote a letter to Joab and sent it by the hand of Uriah. ¹⁵ And he wrote in the letter, saying, "Set Uriah in the forefront of the hottest battle, and retreat from him, that he may be struck down and die." ¹⁶ So it was, while Joab besieged the city, that he assigned Uriah to a place where he knew there were valiant men. ¹⁷ Then the men of the city came out and fought with Joab. And some of the people of the servants of David fell; and Uriah the Hittite died also.

²⁶ When the wife of Uriah heard that Uriah her husband was dead, she mourned for her husband. ²⁷ And when her mourning was over, David sent and brought her to his house, and she became his wife and bore him a son. But the thing that David had done displeased the LORD.

How far are you willing to go against God's will to fulfill your desires?

_____
_____
_____
_____
_____

My thoughts about this scripture

_____
_____
_____
_____
_____
_____
_____
_____

Day 306

Revelation 9 (New King James Version)

Then the fifth angel sounded: And I saw a star fallen from heaven to the earth. To him was given the key to the bottomless pit. [2] And he opened the bottomless pit, and smoke arose out of the pit like the smoke of a great furnace. So the sun and the air were darkened because of the smoke of the pit. [3] Then out of the smoke locusts came upon the earth. And to them was given power, as the scorpions of the earth have power. [4] They were commanded not to harm the grass of the earth, or any green thing, or any tree, but only those men who do not have the seal of God on their foreheads. [5] And they were not given authority to kill them, but to torment them for five months. Their torment was like the torment of a scorpion when it strikes a man. [6] In those days men will seek death and will not find it; they will desire to die, and death will flee from them.

My thoughts about this scripture

_____
_____
_____
_____
_____
_____
_____
_____
_____
_____

Do you know how to avoid encountering this type torment?

_____
_____

I guess the only thing to do now is tell someone else how to avoid it, right?

_____
_____

Day 307

Revelation 22 (New King James Version)

And he showed me a pure[a] river of water of life, clear as crystal, proceeding from the throne of God and of the Lamb. [2] In the middle of its street, and on either side of the river, was the tree of life, which bore twelve fruits, each tree yielding its fruit every month. The leaves of the tree were for the healing of the nations. [3] And there shall be no more curse, but the throne of God and of the Lamb shall be in it, and His servants shall serve Him. [4] They shall see His face, and His name shall be on their foreheads. [5] There shall be no night there: They need no lamp nor light of the sun, for the Lord God gives them light. And they shall reign forever and ever.

My thoughts about this scripture

_____
_____
_____
_____
_____
_____
_____
_____
_____

So do you know how to get to this river?

_____
_____
_____
_____

So, I guess the only thing to do now is tell someone else how to get there, right?

_____
_____

The Book of Proverbs

1. Solomon the son of _____, king of Israel.
   A. Moses
   B. Joshua
   C. Jacob
   D. David

2. The Book of Proverbs can be found where?
   A. New testament
   B. Old testament
   C. Both
   D. Neither

The Book of Esther

1. Queen _____ made a feast for the women in the royal palace. (1:9)
   A. Vashti
   B. Esther
   C. Naomi
   D. Bathsheba

2. Esther is the number ___ book of the Bible.
   A. 17th
   B. 12th
   C. 9th
   D. 25th

Day 309

Luke 23 (New King James Version)

39 Then one of the criminals who were hanged blasphemed Him, saying, "If You are the Christ,[i] save Yourself and us."

40 But the other, answering, rebuked him, saying, "Do you not even fear God, seeing you are under the same condemnation? 41 And we indeed justly, for we receive the due reward of our deeds; but this Man has done nothing wrong." 42 Then he said to Jesus, "Lord,[k] remember me when You come into Your kingdom."

43 And Jesus said to him, "Assuredly, I say to you, today you will be with Me in Paradise."

My thoughts about this scripture

_____
_____
_____
_____
_____
_____

Isn't it great that Jesus, dying himself, was still concerned about this man's soul being saved?

_____
_____
_____
_____
_____

Day 310

1 John 1 (New King James Version)

That which was from the beginning, which we have heard, which we have seen with our eyes, which we have looked upon, and our hands have handled, concerning the Word of life— ² the life was manifested, and we have seen, and bear witness, and declare to you that eternal life which was with the Father and was manifested to us— ³ that which we have seen and heard we declare to you, that you also may have fellowship with us; and truly our fellowship is with the Father and with His Son Jesus Christ. ⁴ And these things we write to you that your[a] joy may be full.

⁵ This is the message which we have heard from Him and declare to you, that God is light and in Him is no darkness at all. ⁶ If we say that we have fellowship with Him, and walk in darkness, we lie and do not practice the truth. ⁷ But if we walk in the light as He is in the light, we have fellowship with one another, and the blood of Jesus Christ His Son cleanses us from all sin.

⁸ If we say that we have no sin, we deceive ourselves, and the truth is not in us. ⁹ If we confess our sins, He is faithful and just to forgive us our sins and to cleanse us from all unrighteousness. ¹⁰ If we say that we have not sinned, we make Him a liar, and His word is not in us.

My thoughts about this scripture

_____
_____
_____
_____
_____
_____
_____
_____
_____
_____

Day 311

Romans 12 (New King James Version)

I beseech you therefore, brethren, by the mercies of God, that you present your bodies a living sacrifice, holy, acceptable to God, which is your reasonable service. ² And do not be conformed to this world, but be transformed by the renewing of your mind, that you may prove what is that good and acceptable and perfect will of God.

³ For I say, through the grace given to me, to everyone who is among you, not to think of himself more highly than he ought to think, but to think soberly, as God has dealt to each one a measure of faith. ⁴ For as we have many members in one body, but all the members do not have the same function, ⁵ so we, being many, are one body in Christ, and individually members of one another. ⁶ Having then gifts differing according to the grace that is given to us, let us use them: if prophecy, let us prophesy in proportion to our faith;

My thoughts about this scripture

_____
_____
_____
_____
_____
_____
_____

What is meant by "and do not be conformed to this world"?

_____
_____
_____
_____
_____

What attempts are you making to ensure you are not conformed?

_____
_____
_____
_____
_____

Day 312

Matthew 20 (New King James Version)

20 Then the mother of Zebedee's sons came to Him with her sons, kneeling down and asking something from Him.

21 And He said to her, "What do you wish?"

She said to Him, "Grant that these two sons of mine may sit, one on Your right hand and the other on the left, in Your kingdom."

22 But Jesus answered and said, "You do not know what you ask. Are you able to drink the cup that I am about to drink, and be baptized with the baptism that I am baptized with?"[d]

They said to Him, "We are able."

23 So He said to them, "You will indeed drink My cup, and be baptized with the baptism that I am baptized with,[e] but to sit on My right hand and on My left is not Mine to give, but it is for those for whom it is prepared by My Father."

24 And when the ten heard it, they were greatly displeased with the two brothers. 25 But Jesus called them to Himself and said, "You know that the rulers of the Gentiles lord it over them, and those who are great exercise authority over them. 26 Yet it shall not be so among you; but whoever desires to become great among you, let him be your servant. 27 And whoever desires to be first among you, let him be your slave— 28 just as the Son of Man did not come to be served, but to serve, and to give His life a ransom for many."

My thoughts about this scripture

_____
_____
_____
_____
_____
_____
_____
_____
_____
_____

Day 313

Philippians 1 (New King James Version)

27 Only let your conduct be worthy of the gospel of Christ, so that whether I come and see you or am absent, I may hear of your affairs, that you stand fast in one spirit, with one mind striving together for the faith of the gospel, 28 and not in any way terrified by your adversaries, which is to them a proof of perdition, but to you of salvation,[d] and that from God. 29 For to you it has been granted on behalf of Christ, not only to believe in Him, but also to suffer for His sake, 30 having the same conflict which you saw in me and now hear is in me.

My thoughts about this scripture

_____
_____
_____
_____
_____
_____
_____
_____
_____
_____

If you never told anyone you were a believer in Christ, would they know by your conduct? Explain.

_____
_____
_____
_____
_____
_____
_____
_____
_____
_____

Day 314

Complete the following;

Galatians 2 (New King James Version)

17 "But if, _____
_____
18 _____
_____.

Philippians 1:29 (New King James Version)

29 For to _____
_____,

Jonah 2 (New King James Version)

Then Jonah prayed to the LORD his God from the fish's belly. 2 And he said:

" _____
_____.

"Out of the belly of Sheol I cried,
And You heard my voice.

Day 315

John 12 (New King James Version)

Then, six days before the Passover, Jesus came to Bethany, where Lazarus was who had been dead,[a] whom He had raised from the dead. 2 There they made Him a supper; and Martha served, but Lazarus was one of those who sat at the table with Him. 3 Then Mary took a pound of very costly oil of spikenard, anointed the feet of Jesus, and wiped His feet with her hair. And the house was filled with the fragrance of the oil.

4 But one of His disciples, Judas Iscariot, Simon's son, who would betray Him, said, 5 "Why was this fragrant oil not sold for three hundred denarii[b] and given to the poor?" 6 This he said, not that he cared for the poor, but because he was a thief, and had the money box; and he used to take what was put in it.

7 But Jesus said, "Let her alone; she has kept[c] this for the day of My burial. 8 For the poor you have with you always, but Me you do not have always."

Are your motives always good?

_____

_____

_____

_____

_____

Like Judas, have you directed someone in the wrong direction because you knew it would benefit you later?

_____

_____

_____

My thoughts about this scripture

_____

_____

_____

_____

_____

_____

_____

Day 316

May your day, your life and your heart be filled with Faith

Hebrews 11 (New King James Version)

Now faith is the substance of things hoped for, the evidence of things not seen. ² *For by it the elders obtained a good testimony.*

³ *By faith we understand that the worlds were framed by the word of God, so that the things which are seen were not made of things which are visible.*

Faith at the Dawn of History

⁴ *By faith Abel offered to God a more excellent sacrifice than Cain, through which he obtained witness that he was righteous, God testifying of his gifts; and through it he being dead still speaks.*

⁵ *By faith Enoch was taken away so that he did not see death, "and was not found, because God had taken him"; [a] for before he was taken he had this testimony, that he pleased God.* ⁶ *But without faith it is impossible to please Him, for he who comes to God must believe that He is, and that He is a rewarder of those who diligently seek Him.*

⁷ *By faith Noah, being divinely warned of things not yet seen, moved with godly fear, prepared an ark for the saving of his household, by which he condemned the world and became heir of the righteousness which is according to faith.*

¹³ *These all died in faith, not having received the promises, but having seen them afar off were assured of them,[c] embraced them and confessed that they were strangers and pilgrims on the earth.* ¹⁴ *For those who say such things declare plainly that they seek a homeland.* ¹⁵ *And truly if they had called to mind that country from which they had come out, they would have had opportunity to return.* ¹⁶ *But now they desire a better, that is, a heavenly country. Therefore God is not ashamed to be called their God, for He has prepared a city for them.*

Day 317

Hebrews 12 (New King James Version)

³ For consider Him who endured such hostility from sinners against Himself, lest you become weary and discouraged in your souls. ⁴ You have not yet resisted to bloodshed, striving against sin. ⁵ And you have forgotten the exhortation which speaks to you as to sons:

"My son, do not despise the chastening of the LORD,
Nor be discouraged when you are rebuked by Him;
⁶ For whom the LORD loves He chastens,
And scourges every son whom He receives."[a]

⁷ If[b] you endure chastening, God deals with you as with sons; for what son is there whom a father does not chasten? ⁸ But if you are without chastening, of which all have become partakers, then you are illegitimate and not sons. ⁹ Furthermore, we have had human fathers who corrected us, and we paid them respect. Shall we not much more readily be in subjection to the Father of spirits and live? ¹⁰ For they indeed for a few days chastened us as seemed best to them, but He for our profit, that we may be partakers of His holiness. ¹¹ Now no chastening seems to be joyful for the present, but painful; nevertheless, afterward it yields the peaceable fruit of righteousness to those who have been trained by it.

My thoughts about this scripture

_____
_____
_____
_____
_____
_____
_____

In reading this I couldn't help but think that Jesus who was blameless had to go through some things, so why do we sometimes feel we shouldn't have to deal with any chastening?

_____
_____
_____
_____
_____
_____
_____

Day 318

2 Timothy 2 (New King James Version)

You therefore, my son, be strong in the grace that is in Christ Jesus. ² And the things that you have heard from me among many witnesses, commit these to faithful men who will be able to teach others also. ³ You therefore must endure[a] hardship as a good soldier of Jesus Christ. ⁴ No one engaged in warfare entangles himself with the affairs of this life, that he may please him who enlisted him as a soldier. ⁵ And also if anyone competes in athletics, he is not crowned unless he competes according to the rules. ⁶ The hardworking farmer must be first to partake of the crops. ⁷ Consider what I say, and may[b] the Lord give you understanding in all things.

⁸ Remember that Jesus Christ, of the seed of David, was raised from the dead according to my gospel, ⁹ for which I suffer trouble as an evildoer, even to the point of chains; but the word of God is not chained. ¹⁰ Therefore I endure all things for the sake of the elect, that they also may obtain the salvation which is in Christ Jesus with eternal glory.

¹¹ This is a faithful saying:

For if we died with Him,
We shall also live with Him.
¹² If we endure,
We shall also reign with Him.
If we deny Him,
He also will deny us.
¹³ If we are faithless,
He remains faithful;
He cannot deny Himself.

My thoughts about this scripture

_____
_____
_____
_____
_____
_____
_____
_____
_____
_____

Day 319

Romans 1 (New King James Version)

18 For the wrath of God is revealed from heaven against all ungodliness and unrighteousness of men, who suppress the truth in unrighteousness, 19 because what may be known of God is manifest in them, for God has shown it to them. 20 For since the creation of the world His invisible attributes are clearly seen, being understood by the things that are made, even His eternal power and Godhead, so that they are without excuse, 21 because, although they knew God, they did not glorify Him as God, nor were thankful, but became futile in their thoughts, and their foolish hearts were darkened. 22 Professing to be wise, they became fools, 23 and changed the glory of the incorruptible God into an image made like corruptible man—and birds and four-footed animals and creeping things.

24 Therefore God also gave them up to uncleanness, in the lusts of their hearts, to dishonor their bodies among themselves, 25 who exchanged the truth of God for the lie, and worshiped and served the creature rather than the Creator, who is blessed forever. Amen.

26 For this reason God gave them up to vile passions. For even their women exchanged the natural use for what is against nature. 27 Likewise also the men, leaving the natural use of the woman, burned in their lust for one another, men with men committing what is shameful, and receiving in themselves the penalty of their error which was due.

28 And even as they did not like to retain God in their knowledge, God gave them over to a debased mind, to do those things which are not fitting; 29 being filled with all unrighteousness, sexual immorality,[c] wickedness, covetousness, maliciousness; full of envy, murder, strife, deceit, evil-mindedness; they are whisperers, 30 backbiters, haters of God, violent, proud, boasters, inventors of evil things, disobedient to parents, 31 undiscerning, untrustworthy, unloving, unforgiving,[d] unmerciful; 32 who, knowing the righteous judgment of God, that those who practice such things are deserving of death, not only do the same but also approve of those who practice them.

My thoughts about this scripture

_____
_____
_____
_____
_____
_____
_____
_____
_____
_____

The Book of 2 Samuel

1. Who was Bathsheba?
    A. The daughter of Eliam and David's sister
    B. The sister of Uriah and the wife of Eliam
    C. A woman bathing that David desired
    D. A woman at the well that Jesus asked to give him water

2. Uriah died by _____.
    A. Killing himself because he dishonored his family
    B. Being trampled by oxen as they stampeded
    C. Being poisoned by his wife because she loved another man
    D. Being sent to fight on the front line of battle

3. Who did God send to confront David about his sin?
    A. Saul
    B. Nathan
    C. Uriah
    D. Solomon

4. What was the punishment for David's sin?
    A. His son died
    B. His wife died
    C. He lost his kingdom
    D. He became very ill for weeks

5. Who was Tamar?
    A. Absalom's sister
    B. Joab's cousin
    C. David's sister
    D. David's youngest wife

6. Absalom sent for Joab twice but he would not come. How did Absalom finally get Joab to come to his house?
    A. Set his barley fields on fire
    B. Stole some of his sheep and donkeys
    C. Sent him food and wine
    D. Offered him money and one of his daughters as a wife

Day 321

2 Samuel 12 (New King James Version)

Then the LORD sent Nathan to David. And he came to him, and said to him: "There were two men in one city, one rich and the other poor. ² The rich man had exceedingly many flocks and herds. ³ But the poor man had nothing, except one little ewe lamb which he had bought and nourished; and it grew up together with him and with his children. It ate of his own food and drank from his own cup and lay in his bosom; and it was like a daughter to him. ⁴ And a traveler came to the rich man, who refused to take from his own flock and from his own herd to prepare one for the wayfaring man who had come to him; but he took the poor man's lamb and prepared it for the man who had come to him."

⁵ So David's anger was greatly aroused against the man, and he said to Nathan, "As the LORD lives, the man who has done this shall surely die! ⁶ And he shall restore fourfold for the lamb, because he did this thing and because he had no pity."

⁷ Then Nathan said to David, "You are the man! Thus says the LORD God of Israel: 'I anointed you king over Israel, and I delivered you from the hand of Saul. ⁸ I gave you your master's house and your master's wives into your keeping, and gave you the house of Israel and Judah. And if that had been too little, I also would have given you much more! ⁹ Why have you despised the commandment of the LORD, to do evil in His sight? You have killed Uriah the Hittite with the sword; you have taken his wife to be your wife, and have killed him with the sword of the people of Ammon. ¹⁰ Now therefore, the sword shall never depart from your house, because you have despised Me, and have taken the wife of Uriah the Hittite to be your wife.' ¹¹ Thus says the LORD: 'Behold, I will raise up adversity against you from your own house; and I will take your wives before your eyes and give them to your neighbor, and he shall lie with your wives in the sight of this sun. ¹² For you did it secretly, but I will do this thing before all Israel, before the sun.'"

¹³ So David said to Nathan, "I have sinned against the LORD."

Do you believe men and women of power and wealth sin because they are usually not confronted?

_____

My thoughts about this scripture

_____
_____
_____
_____
_____

Day 322

Genesis 42 (New King James Version)

⁶ Now Joseph was governor over the land; and it was he who sold to all the people of the land. And Joseph's brothers came and bowed down before him with their faces to the earth. ⁷ Joseph saw his brothers and recognized them, but he acted as a stranger to them and spoke roughly to them. Then he said to them, "Where do you come from?"

And they said, "From the land of Canaan to buy food."

⁸ So Joseph recognized his brothers, but they did not recognize him. ⁹ Then Joseph remembered the dreams which he had dreamed about them, and said to them, "You are spies! You have come to see the nakedness of the land!"

My thoughts about this scripture

_____
_____
_____
_____
_____
_____
_____
_____

Have you ever mistreated someone and were put in a situation where you needed them later and that was the only person who could help you?

_____
_____

Do you think you know why you needed them?

_____
_____
_____

Did it change the way you felt about them? Why?

_____
_____
_____
_____

Day 323

Exodus 7 (New King James Version)

[8] Then the LORD spoke to Moses and Aaron, saying, [9] "When Pharaoh speaks to you, saying, 'Show a miracle for yourselves,' then you shall say to Aaron, 'Take your rod and cast it before Pharaoh, and let it become a serpent.'" [10] So Moses and Aaron went in to Pharaoh, and they did so, just as the LORD commanded. And Aaron cast down his rod before Pharaoh and before his servants, and it became a serpent.

[11] But Pharaoh also called the wise men and the sorcerers; so the magicians of Egypt, they also did in like manner with their enchantments. [12] For every man threw down his rod, and they became serpents. But Aaron's rod swallowed up their rods. [13] And Pharaoh's heart grew hard, and he did not heed them, as the LORD had said.

Have you ever tried to follow God's word but there were people around trying to show you another way?

_____
_____
_____

My thoughts about this scripture

_____
_____
_____
_____
_____
_____

Moses and Aaron were following God's direction although it seemed very difficult. Do you continue to do what you know to be right even when it becomes difficult?

_____
_____
_____
_____

Day 324

Mark 13 (New King James Version)

³ Now as He sat on the Mount of Olives opposite the temple, Peter, James, John, and Andrew asked Him privately, ⁴ "Tell us, when will these things be? And what will be the sign when all these things will be fulfilled?"

⁵ And Jesus, answering them, began to say: "Take heed that no one deceives you. ⁶ For many will come in My name, saying, 'I am He,' and will deceive many. ⁷ But when you hear of wars and rumors of wars, do not be troubled; for such things must happen, but the end is not yet. ⁸ For nation will rise against nation, and kingdom against kingdom. And there will be earthquakes in various places, and there will be famines and troubles.[a] These are the beginnings of sorrows.

⁹ "But watch out for yourselves, for they will deliver you up to councils, and you will be beaten in the synagogues. You will be brought[b] before rulers and kings for My sake, for a testimony to them. ¹⁰ And the gospel must first be preached to all the nations. ¹¹ But when they arrest you and deliver you up, do not worry beforehand, or premeditate[c] what you will speak. But whatever is given you in that hour, speak that; for it is not you who speak, but the Holy Spirit. ¹² Now brother will betray brother to death, and a father his child; and children will rise up against parents and cause them to be put to death. ¹³ And you will be hated by all for My name's sake. But he who endures to the end shall be saved.

Do you think that much of what Jesus described is happening now? Explain.

_____
_____
_____
_____
_____
_____

Are you taking the correct steps to ensure no one deceives you?

_____

What are some of the things you are doing?

_____
_____
_____
_____
_____

Day 325

Deuteronomy 8 (New King James Version)

"Every commandment which I command you today you must be careful to observe, that you may live and multiply, and go in and possess the land of which the LORD swore to your fathers. [2] And you shall remember that the LORD your God led you all the way these forty years in the wilderness, to humble you and test you, to know what was in your heart, whether you would keep His commandments or not. [3] So He humbled you, allowed you to hunger, and fed you with manna which you did not know nor did your fathers know, that He might make you know that man shall not live by bread alone; but man lives by every word that proceeds from the mouth of the LORD. [4] Your garments did not wear out on you, nor did your foot swell these forty years. [5] You should know in your heart that as a man chastens his son, so the LORD your God chastens you.

My thoughts about this scripture

_____
_____
_____
_____
_____
_____
_____
_____

Aren't you glad God judges us by our heart and not by everything we do?

_____
_____
_____
_____

Now this doesn't mean you can do whatever you want as long as you feel bad about it later. You have to make sincere efforts to do what is right as well as feel in your heart what is right. Once you allow the Holy Spirit to lead you, your actions and your heart will begin to work together. You just have to get out of your own way and allow yourself to be led.

Isn't God Great!?

Day 326

Write about a recent day when things were not going so well for you. While you're writing, include a scripture that helped you get through it.

One day I....

_____
_____
_____
_____
_____
_____
_____
_____
_____
_____
_____

Was the scripture one you knew or was it shown to you in the mist of your issue?

_____
_____
_____

What was your reaction when you read the scripture?

_____
_____
_____

God's word may not always make what we are going through go away at the moment but if you truly focus on the word and where that word is coming from, it will help you get through it and if you allow it, will help you avoid going through it again.

Have you memorized any scripture that you keep with you just in case? If so write it below, if not find one (or two) and write it below.

_____
_____
_____
_____
_____
_____
_____
_____

Day 327

Exodus 16 (New King James Version)

And Moses said to them, "This is the bread which the LORD has given you to eat. ¹⁶ This is the thing which the LORD has commanded: 'Let every man gather it according to each one's need, one omer for each person, according to the number of persons; let every man take for those who are in his tent.'"

¹⁷ Then the children of Israel did so and gathered, some more, some less. ¹⁸ So when they measured it by omers, he who gathered much had nothing left over, and he who gathered little had no lack. Every man had gathered according to each one's need. ¹⁹ And Moses said, "Let no one leave any of it till morning." ²⁰ Notwithstanding they did not heed Moses. But some of them left part of it until morning, and it bred worms and stank. And Moses was angry with them. ²¹ So they gathered it every morning, every man according to his need. And when the sun became hot, it melted.

As they prayed (well complained) to God, He heard them and provided yet they still did not follow His direction. Why do you think it is so hard for us to just follow God completely?

_____
_____
_____
_____
_____
_____

Going for a long time and not having can lead to selfishness and greed. How do you keep yourself obedient after God has blessed you and not allow that blessing to condemn you?

_____
_____
_____
_____
_____

Day 328

Psalm 138 (New King James Version)

I will praise You with my whole heart;
Before the gods I will sing praises to You.
² I will worship toward Your holy temple,
And praise Your name
For Your lovingkindness and Your truth;
For You have magnified Your word above all Your name.
³ In the day when I cried out, You answered me,
And made me bold with strength in my soul.

⁴ All the kings of the earth shall praise You, O Lord,
When they hear the words of Your mouth.
⁵ Yes, they shall sing of the ways of the Lord,
For great is the glory of the Lord.
⁶ Though the Lord is on high,
Yet He regards the lowly;
But the proud He knows from afar.

⁷ Though I walk in the midst of trouble, You will revive me;
You will stretch out Your hand
Against the wrath of my enemies,
And Your right hand will save me.
⁸ The Lord will perfect that which concerns me;
Your mercy, O Lord, endures forever;
Do not forsake the works of Your hands

My thoughts about this scripture

_____
_____
_____
_____
_____
_____
_____
_____
_____
_____

Day 329

Revelation 20 (New King James Version)

⁷ Now when the thousand years have expired, Satan will be released from his prison ⁸ and will go out to deceive the nations which are in the four corners of the earth, Gog and Magog, to gather them together to battle, whose number is as the sand of the sea. ⁹ They went up on the breadth of the earth and surrounded the camp of the saints and the beloved city. And fire came down from God out of heaven and devoured them. ¹⁰ The devil, who deceived them, was cast into the lake of fire and brimstone where[b] the beast and the false prophet are. And they will be tormented day and night forever and ever.

My thoughts about this scripture

_____
_____
_____
_____
_____
_____
_____
_____
_____

If you knew for sure a team was going to lose the game would you bet on them?

_____
_____

If the Bible tells us that good triumphs over evil, why are still following evil? Why are you so set on playing for a losing team? Especially when the loser is tormented?

_____
_____
_____
_____
_____
_____
_____

Day 330

2 Chronicles 10 (New King James Version)

⁶ Then King Rehoboam consulted the elders who stood before his father Solomon while he still lived, saying, "How do you advise me to answer these people?"

⁷ And they spoke to him, saying, "If you are kind to these people, and please them, and speak good words to them, they will be your servants forever."

⁸ But he rejected the advice which the elders had given him, and consulted the young men who had grown up with him, who stood before him. ⁹ And he said to them, "What advice do you give? How should we answer this people who have spoken to me, saying, 'Lighten the yoke which your father put on us'?"

¹⁰ Then the young men who had grown up with him spoke to him, saying, "Thus you should speak to the people who have spoken to you, saying, 'Your father made our yoke heavy, but you make it lighter on us'—thus you shall say to them: 'My little finger shall be thicker than my father's waist! ¹¹ And now, whereas my father put a heavy yoke on you, I will add to your yoke; my father chastised you with whips, but I will chastise you with scourges!'"[a]

Why is it we always seek advice from the worse sources? We turn to our boys who situation isn't as good as ours, their stability isn't as good as ours and their walk with Christ isn't as good as ours. Yet, we seek counsel with them.

From whom do you seek your counsel? Why?

_____
_____
_____
_____
_____

How do you avoid giving and getting bad advice?

_____
_____
_____
_____
_____

Day 331

Psalm 53 (New King James Version)

The fool has said in his heart,
"There is no God."
They are corrupt, and have done abominable iniquity;
There is none who does good.

² God looks down from heaven upon the children of men,
To see if there are any who understand, who seek God.
³ Every one of them has turned aside;
They have together become corrupt;
There is none who does good,
No, not one.

⁴ Have the workers of iniquity no knowledge,
Who eat up my people as they eat bread,
And do not call upon God?
⁵ There they are in great fear
Where no fear was,
For God has scattered the bones of him who encamps against you;
You have put them to shame,
Because God has despised them.

⁶ Oh, that the salvation of Israel would come out of Zion!
When God brings back the captivity of His people,
Let Jacob rejoice and Israel be glad.

My thoughts about this scripture

_____
_____
_____
_____
_____
_____
_____
_____

Day 332

Hosea 13 (New King James Version)

⁴ "Yet I am the L<small>ORD</small> your God
Ever since the land of Egypt,
And you shall know no God but Me;
For there is no savior besides Me.
⁵ I knew you in the wilderness,
In the land of great drought.
⁶ When they had pasture, they were filled;
They were filled and their heart was exalted;
Therefore they forgot Me.

⁷ "So I will be to them like a lion;
Like a leopard by the road I will lurk;
⁸ I will meet them like a bear deprived of her cubs;
I will tear open their rib cage,
And there I will devour them like a lion.
The wild beast shall tear them.

⁹ "O Israel, you are destroyed,[b]
But your help[c] is from Me.
¹⁰ I will be your King;[d]
Where is any other,
That he may save you in all your cities?
And your judges to whom you said,
'Give me a king and princes'?
¹¹ I gave you a king in My anger,
And took him away in My wrath.

My thoughts about this scripture

_____
_____
_____
_____
_____
_____
_____

Day 333

Genesis 50 (New King James Version)

15 When Joseph's brothers saw that their father was dead, they said, "Perhaps Joseph will hate us, and may actually repay us for all the evil which we did to him." 16 So they sent messengers to Joseph, saying, "Before your father died he commanded, saying, 17 'Thus you shall say to Joseph: "I beg you, please forgive the trespass of your brothers and their sin; for they did evil to you."' Now, please, forgive the trespass of the servants of the God of your father." And Joseph wept when they spoke to him.

18 Then his brothers also went and fell down before his face, and they said, "Behold, we are your servants."

19 Joseph said to them, "Do not be afraid, for am I in the place of God? 20 But as for you, you meant evil against me; but God meant it for good, in order to bring it about as it is this day, to save many people alive. 21 Now therefore, do not be afraid; I will provide for you and your little ones." And he comforted them and spoke kindly to them.

My thoughts about this scripture

_____
_____
_____
_____
_____
_____
_____
_____
_____

Have you forgiven those who have mistreated you?

_____
_____
_____

Day 334

Job 25 (New King James Version)

Then Bildad the Shuhite answered and said:

[2] "Dominion and fear belong to Him;
He makes peace in His high places.
[3] Is there any number to His armies?
Upon whom does His light not rise?
[4] How then can man be righteous before God?
Or how can he be pure who is born of a woman?
[5] If even the moon does not shine,
And the stars are not pure in His sight,
[6] How much less man, who is a maggot,
And a son of man, who is a worm?"

What is meant by "Dominion and fear belong to Him"?

_____
_____
_____
_____

Do you believe man can be righteous before God? Explain.

_____
_____
_____
_____
_____
_____

Day 335

Psalm 62 (New King James Version)

Truly my soul silently waits for God;
From Him comes my salvation.
² He only is my rock and my salvation;
He is my defense;
I shall not be greatly moved.

⁶ He only is my rock and my salvation;
He is my defense;
I shall not be moved.
⁷ In God is my salvation and my glory;
The rock of my strength,
And my refuge, is in God.

¹¹ God has spoken once,
Twice I have heard this:
That power belongs to God.
¹² Also to You, O Lord, belongs mercy;
For You render to each one according to his work.

My thoughts about this scripture

_____
_____
_____
_____
_____
_____
_____
_____

Day 336

Matthew 22 (New King James Version)

¹⁵ Then the Pharisees went and plotted how they might entangle Him in His talk. ¹⁶ And they sent to Him their disciples with the Herodians, saying, "Teacher, we know that You are true, and teach the way of God in truth; nor do You care about anyone, for You do not regard the person of men. ¹⁷ Tell us, therefore, what do You think? Is it lawful to pay taxes to Caesar, or not?"

¹⁸ But Jesus perceived their wickedness, and said, "Why do you test Me, you hypocrites? ¹⁹ Show Me the tax money."

So they brought Him a denarius.

²⁰ And He said to them, "Whose image and inscription is this?"

²¹ They said to Him, "Caesar's."

And He said to them, "Render therefore to Caesar the things that are Caesar's, and to God the things that are God's." ²² When they had heard these words, they marveled, and left Him and went their way.

Do you spend time trying to find fault in Christ to justify not following His will?

_____
_____
_____
_____
_____

My thoughts about this scripture

_____
_____
_____
_____
_____
_____
_____

Day 237

Jude 1 (New King James Version)

⁵ But I want to remind you, though you once knew this, that the Lord, having saved the people out of the land of Egypt, afterward destroyed those who did not believe. ⁶ And the angels who did not keep their proper domain, but left their own abode, He has reserved in everlasting chains under darkness for the judgment of the great day; ⁷ as Sodom and Gomorrah, and the cities around them in a similar manner to these, having given themselves over to sexual immorality and gone after strange flesh, are set forth as an example, suffering the vengeance of eternal fire.

⁸ Likewise also these dreamers defile the flesh, reject authority, and speak evil of dignitaries. ⁹ Yet Michael the archangel, in contending with the devil, when he disputed about the body of Moses, dared not bring against him a reviling accusation, but said, "The Lord rebuke you!" ¹⁰ But these speak evil of whatever they do not know; and whatever they know naturally, like brute beasts, in these things they corrupt themselves. ¹¹ Woe to them! For they have gone in the way of Cain, have run greedily in the error of Balaam for profit, and perished in the rebellion of Korah.

My thoughts about this scripture

_____
_____
_____
_____
_____
_____
_____
_____
_____

If you are truly a believer, why haven't you changed your evil ways?

_____
_____
_____
_____
_____

Sometimes we assume we have changed, ask someone you trust.

Day 338

New Testament

```
P  B  N  L  V  Y  V  O  O  W  R  K  P  D  N
H  U  O  O  R  E  T  E  P  E  U  J  R  H  E
I  R  M  Z  M  E  S  G  V  H  X  V  O  A  T
L  K  O  Q  C  E  J  E  D  T  M  J  B  L  M
I  Z  W  M  P  O  L  E  D  T  T  D  D  T  N
P  E  G  Z  A  A  R  I  D  A  B  Q  V  U  U
P  K  V  K  T  N  S  I  H  M  J  F  Z  A  H
I  U  B  I  Y  V  S  C  N  P  E  G  F  I  M
A  L  O  L  P  O  T  J  L  T  B  N  O  O  Y
N  N  T  T  F  W  P  D  I  W  H  Q  C  H  T
S  S  N  A  I  S  S  O  L  O  C  I  T  J  I
H  E  B  R  E  W  S  U  Y  J  D  O  A  Y  T
S  N  Q  W  W  M  Q  O  G  L  M  M  X  N  U
N  Z  L  A  C  T  S  O  T  I  E  B  L  P  S
G  R  F  F  U  B  J  E  T  S  Y  Z  S  C  K
```

ACTS   COLOSSIANS   CORINTHIANS
HEBREWS   JAMES   JOHN
LUKE   MARK   MATTHEW
PETER   PHILEMON   PHILIPPIANS
REVELATION   ROMANS   TIMOTHY
TITUS

Day 339

Romans 10 (New King James Version)

Brethren, my heart's desire and prayer to God for Israel[a] is that they may be saved. [2] For I bear them witness that they have a zeal for God, but not according to knowledge. [3] For they being ignorant of God's righteousness, and seeking to establish their own righteousness, have not submitted to the righteousness of God. [4] For Christ is the end of the law for righteousness to everyone who believes.

[5] For Moses writes about the righteousness which is of the law, "The man who does those things shall live by them."[b] [6] But the righteousness of faith speaks in this way, "Do not say in your heart, 'Who will ascend into heaven?'"[c] (that is, to bring Christ down from above) [7] or, "'Who will descend into the abyss?'"[d] (that is, to bring Christ up from the dead). [8] But what does it say? "The word is near you, in your mouth and in your heart"[e] (that is, the word of faith which we preach): [9] that if you confess with your mouth the Lord Jesus and believe in your heart that God has raised Him from the dead, you will be saved. [10] For with the heart one believes unto righteousness, and with the mouth confession is made unto salvation. [11] For the Scripture says, "Whoever believes on Him will not be put to shame."[f] [12] For there is no distinction between Jew and Greek, for the same Lord over all is rich to all who call upon Him. [13] For "whoever calls on the name of the LORD shall be saved."[g]

Do you pray in your heart that others are saved?

_____

_____

Are the only people you pray for family or people you know are praying for you?

_____

_____

When is the last time you prayed for a stranger? An enemy?

_____

_____

_____

_____

To believe in your heart and to pray just as hard for others as you do for yourself is difficult sometimes. How do you ensure you continue to do both?

_____

_____

_____

Day 340

Review:

1. Name the first five books of the Bible
   A.
   B.
   C.
   D.
   E.

2. In Exodus, where did Moses lead his people out of?
   _____

3. David had a man killed so he could have his wife, what was her name?
   _____

4. In Acts 14:14, who was the apostle with Paul?
   _____

5. Finish the following; (Matthew 12:33)

   [33] "Either make the tree _____
   _____.

6. In Jonah 1:17, where was Johan for three days and three nights?
   _____

7. In Genesis 10:1, what were the names of Noah's sons?
   _____   _____   _____

8. Write John 3:16 below, write as much as you can without looking in your bible.
   _____
   _____
   _____
   _____
   _____
   _____

Day 341

Luke 1 (New King James Version)

²⁹ But when she saw him,[d] she was troubled at his saying, and considered what manner of greeting this was. ³⁰ Then the angel said to her, "Do not be afraid, Mary, for you have found favor with God. ³¹ And behold, you will conceive in your womb and bring forth a Son, and shall call His name JESUS. ³² He will be great, and will be called the Son of the Highest; and the Lord God will give Him the throne of His father David. ³³ And He will reign over the house of Jacob forever, and of His kingdom there will be no end."

³⁴ Then Mary said to the angel, "How can this be, since I do not know a man?"

³⁵ And the angel answered and said to her, "The Holy Spirit will come upon you, and the power of the Highest will overshadow you; therefore, also, that Holy One who is to be born will be called the Son of God. ³⁶ Now indeed, Elizabeth your relative has also conceived a son in her old age; and this is now the sixth month for her who was called barren. ³⁷ For with God nothing will be impossible."

³⁸ Then Mary said, "Behold the maidservant of the Lord! Let it be to me according to your word." And the angel departed from her.

My thoughts about this scripture

_____
_____
_____
_____
_____
_____
_____
_____
_____
_____

Day 342

Exodus 17 (New King James Version)

Then all the congregation of the children of Israel set out on their journey from the Wilderness of Sin, according to the commandment of the LORD, and camped in Rephidim; but there was no water for the people to drink. ^{2} *Therefore the people contended with Moses, and said, "Give us water, that we may drink."*

So Moses said to them, "Why do you contend with me? Why do you tempt the LORD?"

^{3} *And the people thirsted there for water, and the people complained against Moses, and said, "Why is it you have brought us up out of Egypt, to kill us and our children and our livestock with thirst?"*

^{4} *So Moses cried out to the LORD, saying, "What shall I do with this people? They are almost ready to stone me!"*

^{5} *And the LORD said to Moses, "Go on before the people, and take with you some of the elders of Israel. Also take in your hand your rod with which you struck the river, and go.* ^{6} *Behold, I will stand before you there on the rock in Horeb; and you shall strike the rock, and water will come out of it, that the people may drink."*

And Moses did so in the sight of the elders of Israel. ^{7} *So he called the name of the place Massah*[a] *and Meribah,*[b] *because of the contention of the children of Israel, and because they tempted the LORD, saying, "Is the LORD among us or not?"*

When things are not going so well for you, do you question if God is with you?

_____

_____

_____

Is it possible to be in the middle of a blessing and spend so much time complaining that you don't realize it?

_____

_____

_____

_____

_____

_____

Day 343

Genesis 28 (New King James Version)

³ "May God Almighty bless you,
And make you fruitful and multiply you,
That you may be an assembly of peoples;
⁴ And give you the blessing of Abraham,
To you and your descendants with you,
That you may inherit the land
In which you are a stranger,
Which God gave to Abraham."

What do you think is meant by *"inherit the land in which you are a stranger"*?

_____
_____
_____
_____
_____
_____

We have been promised a gift by someone who cannot lie, are you happy about that?

_____
_____
_____
_____
_____

Are you preparing to receive that gift? Explain how.

_____
_____
_____
_____
_____
_____
_____
_____
_____

Day 344

Acts 23 (New King James Version)

Then Paul, looking earnestly at the council, said, "Men and brethren, I have lived in all good conscience before God until this day." [2] And the high priest Ananias commanded those who stood by him to strike him on the mouth. [3] Then Paul said to him, "God will strike you, you whitewashed wall! For you sit to judge me according to the law, and do you command me to be struck contrary to the law?"

[4] And those who stood by said, "Do you revile God's high priest?"

[5] Then Paul said, "I did not know, brethren, that he was the high priest; for it is written, 'You shall not speak evil of a ruler of your people.'"[a]

Without getting too political, do you abide by the last verse of this scripture?

_____
_____
_____
_____

Do you pray for all our leaders?

_____
_____

My thoughts about this scripture

_____
_____
_____
_____
_____
_____
_____
_____
_____

Day 345

Zechariah 5 (New King James Version)

Then I turned and raised my eyes, and saw there a flying scroll.

² And he said to me, "What do you see?"

So I answered, "I see a flying scroll. Its length is twenty cubits and its width ten cubits."

³ Then he said to me, "This is the curse that goes out over the face of the whole earth: 'Every thief shall be expelled,' according to this side of the scroll; and, 'Every perjurer shall be expelled,' according to that side of it."

⁴ "I will send out the curse," says the LORD of hosts;
"It shall enter the house of the thief
And the house of the one who swears falsely by My name.
It shall remain in the midst of his house
And consume it, with its timber and stones."

My thoughts about this scripture

_____
_____
_____
_____
_____
_____
_____
_____
_____
_____

Day 346

Titus 3 (New King James Version)

Remind them to be subject to rulers and authorities, to obey, to be ready for every good work, [2] to speak evil of no one, to be peaceable, gentle, showing all humility to all men. [3] For we ourselves were also once foolish, disobedient, deceived, serving various lusts and pleasures, living in malice and envy, hateful and hating one another. [4] But when the kindness and the love of God our Savior toward man appeared, [5] not by works of righteousness which we have done, but according to His mercy He saved us, through the washing of regeneration and renewing of the Holy Spirit, [6] whom He poured out on us abundantly through Jesus Christ our Savior, [7] that having been justified by His grace we should become heirs according to the hope of eternal life.

[8] This is a faithful saying, and these things I want you to affirm constantly, that those who have believed in God should be careful to maintain good works. These things are good and profitable to men.

Do you remember when you were disobedient and deceiving, as you're accusing someone else of being disobedient and deceiving?

_____
_____
_____
_____
_____
_____

My thoughts about this scripture

_____
_____
_____
_____
_____
_____
_____
_____
_____
_____
_____

Day 347

John 6 (New King James Version)

7 Philip answered Him, "Two hundred denarii worth of bread is not sufficient for them, that every one of them may have a little."

8 One of His disciples, Andrew, Simon Peter's brother, said to Him, 9 "There is a lad here who has five barley loaves and two small fish, but what are they among so many?"

10 Then Jesus said, "Make the people sit down." Now there was much grass in the place. So the men sat down, in number about five thousand. 11 And Jesus took the loaves, and when He had given thanks He distributed them to the disciples, and the disciples[a] to those sitting down; and likewise of the fish, as much as they wanted. 12 So when they were filled, He said to His disciples, "Gather up the fragments that remain, so that nothing is lost." 13 Therefore they gathered them up, and filled twelve baskets with the fragments of the five barley loaves which were left over by those who had eaten. 14 Then those men, when they had seen the sign that Jesus did, said, "This is truly the Prophet who is to come into the world."

Have you, like Philip, tried to limit Christ by what you see?

_____
_____
_____
_____
_____

My thoughts about this scripture

_____
_____
_____
_____
_____
_____
_____
_____

Day 348

Colossians 3 (New King James Version)

The Christian Home

[18] Wives, submit to your own husbands, as is fitting in the Lord.

[19] Husbands, love your wives and do not be bitter toward them.

[20] Children, obey your parents in all things, for this is well pleasing to the Lord.

[21] Fathers, do not provoke your children, lest they become discouraged.

[22] Bondservants, obey in all things your masters according to the flesh, not with eyeservice, as men-pleasers, but in sincerity of heart, fearing God. [23] And whatever you do, do it heartily, as to the Lord and not to men, [24] knowing that from the Lord you will receive the reward of the inheritance; for[a] you serve the Lord Christ. [25] But he who does wrong will be repaid for what he has done, and there is no partiality.

Christ provides us with what we need to be a Christian family. Will you incorporate these things into your family? How?

_____

_____

_____

_____

If you do not treat your spouse in this manner and you do not treat your children this way, is it because you are waiting for them to treat you this way first?
Why not be the Christian that will be pleasing to the Lord?

_____

_____

_____

_____

Day 349

Micah 7 (New King James Version)

⁸ Do not rejoice over me, my enemy;
When I fall, I will arise;
When I sit in darkness,
The LORD will be a light to me.
⁹ I will bear the indignation of the LORD,
Because I have sinned against Him,
Until He pleads my case
And executes justice for me.
He will bring me forth to the light;
I will see His righteousness.
¹⁰ Then she who is my enemy will see,
And shame will cover her who said to me,
"Where is the LORD your God?"
My eyes will see her;
Now she will be trampled down
Like mud in the streets.

"When I fall, I will arise", what does that mean to you?

_____
_____
_____
_____
_____

Why do you think nonbelievers are so quick to point out issues of believers?

_____
_____
_____
_____
_____

Day 350

Matthew 14 (New King James Version)

25 Now in the fourth watch of the night Jesus went to them, walking on the sea. 26 And when the disciples saw Him walking on the sea, they were troubled, saying, "It is a ghost!" And they cried out for fear.

27 But immediately Jesus spoke to them, saying, "Be of good cheer! It is I; do not be afraid."

28 And Peter answered Him and said, "Lord, if it is You, command me to come to You on the water."

29 So He said, "Come." And when Peter had come down out of the boat, he walked on the water to go to Jesus. 30 But when he saw that the wind was boisterous,[b] he was afraid; and beginning to sink he cried out, saying, "Lord, save me!"

31 And immediately Jesus stretched out His hand and caught him, and said to him, "O you of little faith, why did you doubt?" 32 And when they got into the boat, the wind ceased.

33 Then those who were in the boat came and[c] worshiped Him, saying, "Truly You are the Son of God."

How strong is your faith?

_____
_____
_____
_____

My thoughts about this scripture

_____
_____
_____
_____
_____
_____
_____
_____

Day 351

Isaiah 33 (New King James Version)

Woe to you who plunder, though you have not been plundered;
And you who deal treacherously, though they have not dealt treacherously with you!
When you cease plundering,
You will be plundered;
When you make an end of dealing treacherously,
They will deal treacherously with you.

2 O Lord, be gracious to us;
We have waited for You.
Be their[a] arm every morning,
Our salvation also in the time of trouble.
3 At the noise of the tumult the people shall flee;
When You lift Yourself up, the nations shall be scattered;
4 And Your plunder shall be gathered
Like the gathering of the caterpillar;
As the running to and fro of locusts,
He shall run upon them.

Do you think *"When you cease plundering, You will be plundered;"* means you get back what you give?

_____
_____
_____
_____
_____

My thoughts about this scripture

_____
_____
_____
_____
_____
_____
_____

Day 352

2 Corinthians 10 (New King James Version)

Now I, Paul, myself am pleading with you by the meekness and gentleness of Christ— who in presence am lowly among you, but being absent am bold toward you. [2] But I beg you that when I am present I may not be bold with that confidence by which I intend to be bold against some, who think of us as if we walked according to the flesh. [3] For though we walk in the flesh, we do not war according to the flesh. [4] For the weapons of our warfare are not carnal but mighty in God for pulling down strongholds, [5] casting down arguments and every high thing that exalts itself against the knowledge of God, bringing every thought into captivity to the obedience of Christ, [6] and being ready to punish all disobedience when your obedience is fulfilled.

My thoughts about this scripture

_____
_____
_____
_____
_____
_____
_____
_____

What is your understanding of walking in flesh but do not war according to the flesh?

_____
_____
_____
_____
_____
_____
_____
_____

Day 353

Answer the following;

1. How did Jonah try to avoid God?

_____
_____
_____

2. Who walks us through the events in Revelation?

_____

3. Although he was blameless, who did God allow Satan to tempt by taking his family and possessions?

_____

4. Name one of the plagues in Exodus.

_____

5. Write a scripture below

_____
_____
_____
_____

6. Why did you choose this scripture

_____
_____
_____

Day 354

Malachi 3 (New King James Version)

⁸ "Will a man rob God?
Yet you have robbed Me!
But you say,
'In what way have we robbed You?'
In tithes and offerings.
⁹ You are cursed with a curse,
For you have robbed Me,
Even this whole nation.
¹⁰ Bring all the tithes into the storehouse,
That there may be food in My house,
And try Me now in this,"
Says the LORD of hosts,
"If I will not open for you the windows of heaven
And pour out for you such blessing
That there will not be room enough to receive it.

Have you trusted God enough to pay your tithes consistently?

_____
_____
_____
_____
_____
_____

Have you ever considered it is not you giving God 10% of your money but Him giving you 90% of His money?

_____
_____
_____
_____
_____
_____
_____

Day 355

Haggai 2 (New King James Version)

[15] 'And now, carefully consider from this day forward: from before stone was laid upon stone in the temple of the LORD— [16] since those days, when one came to a heap of twenty ephahs, there were but ten; when one came to the wine vat to draw out fifty baths from the press, there were but twenty. [17] I struck you with blight and mildew and hail in all the labors of your hands; yet you did not turn to Me,' says the LORD. [18] 'Consider now from this day forward, from the twenty-fourth day of the ninth month, from the day that the foundation of the LORD's temple was laid—consider it: [19] Is the seed still in the barn? As yet the vine, the fig tree, the pomegranate, and the olive tree have not yielded fruit. But from this day I will bless you.'"

My thoughts about this scripture

_____
_____
_____
_____
_____
_____
_____
_____

Day 356

Leviticus 20 (New King James Version)

22 'You shall therefore keep all My statutes and all My judgments, and perform them, that the land where I am bringing you to dwell may not vomit you out. 23 And you shall not walk in the statutes of the nation which I am casting out before you; for they commit all these things, and therefore I abhor them. 24 But I have said to you, "You shall inherit their land, and I will give it to you to possess, a land flowing with milk and honey." I am the LORD your God, who has separated you from the peoples. 25 You shall therefore distinguish between clean animals and unclean, between unclean birds and clean, and you shall not make yourselves abominable by beast or by bird, or by any kind of living thing that creeps on the ground, which I have separated from you as unclean. 26 And you shall be holy to Me, for I the LORD am holy, and have separated you from the peoples, that you should be Mine.

My thoughts about this scripture

_____
_____
_____
_____
_____
_____
_____
_____
_____

Are you making efforts to keep yourself separate from unclean things? Give examples.

_____
_____
_____
_____
_____
_____
_____
_____
_____

Day 357

Ezra 7 (New King James Version)

¹³ I issue a decree that all those of the people of Israel and the priests and Levites in my realm, who volunteer to go up to Jerusalem, may go with you. ¹⁴ And whereas you are being sent by the king and his seven counselors to inquire concerning Judah and Jerusalem, with regard to the Law of your God which is in your hand; ¹⁵ and whereas you are to carry the silver and gold which the king and his counselors have freely offered to the God of Israel, whose dwelling is in Jerusalem; ¹⁶ and whereas all the silver and gold that you may find in all the province of Babylon, along with the freewill offering of the people and the priests, are to be freely offered for the house of their God in Jerusalem— ¹⁷ now therefore, be careful to buy with this money bulls, rams, and lambs, with their grain offerings and their drink offerings, and offer them on the altar of the house of your God in Jerusalem.

¹⁸ And whatever seems good to you and your brethren to do with the rest of the silver and the gold, do it according to the will of your God. ¹⁹ Also the articles that are given to you for the service of the house of your God, deliver in full before the God of Jerusalem. ²⁰ And whatever more may be needed for the house of your God, which you may have occasion to provide, pay for it from the king's treasury.

What are you willing to provide to assist with the will of God?

_____

_____

_____

_____

My thoughts about this scripture

_____

_____

_____

_____

_____

_____

_____

_____

Day 358

Complete the following;

1. Malachi 3 (New King James Version)

[2] *"But who can endure the day of His coming?*
_____
_____
_____.

[3] *He will sit as a refiner and a purifier of*
*silver.*_____
_____
_____

2. 2 Thessalonians 2 (New King James Version)

[16] *Now may our*
_____
_____
_____,

[17] *comfort your -*
_____
_____
_____.

Day 359

2 Thessalonians 2 (New King James Version)

Now, brethren, concerning the coming of our Lord Jesus Christ and our gathering together to Him, we ask you, [2] not to be soon shaken in mind or troubled, either by spirit or by word or by letter, as if from us, as though the day of Christ[a] had come. [3] Let no one deceive you by any means; for that Day will not come unless the falling away comes first, and the man of sin[b] is revealed, the son of perdition, [4] who opposes and exalts himself above all that is called God or that is worshiped, so that he sits as God[c] in the temple of God, showing himself that he is God.

My thoughts about this scripture

_____
_____
_____
_____
_____
_____
_____

What do you think is meant by "*unless the falling away comes first*"?

_____
_____
_____
_____
_____

Day 360

Matthew 9 (New King James Version)

18 While He spoke these things to them, behold, a ruler came and worshiped Him, saying, "My daughter has just died, but come and lay Your hand on her and she will live." 19 So Jesus arose and followed him, and so did His disciples.

20 And suddenly, a woman who had a flow of blood for twelve years came from behind and touched the hem of His garment. 21 For she said to herself, "If only I may touch His garment, I shall be made well." 22 But Jesus turned around, and when He saw her He said, "Be of good cheer, daughter; your faith has made you well." And the woman was made well from that hour.

23 When Jesus came into the ruler's house, and saw the flute players and the noisy crowd wailing, 24 He said to them, "Make room, for the girl is not dead, but sleeping." And they ridiculed Him. 25 But when the crowd was put outside, He went in and took her by the hand, and the girl arose. 26 And the report of this went out into all that land.

By your faith in His power, what will you allow Jesus to heal for you today?

_____
_____
_____
_____
_____
_____
_____

My thought about this scripture

_____
_____
_____
_____
_____
_____

Day 361

2 Kings 23 (New King James Version)

³ Then the king stood by a pillar and made a covenant before the LORD, to follow the LORD and to keep His commandments and His testimonies and His statutes, with all his heart and all his soul, to perform the words of this covenant that were written in this book. And all the people took a stand for the covenant. ⁴ And the king commanded Hilkiah the high priest, the priests of the second order, and the doorkeepers, to bring out of the temple of the LORD all the articles that were made for Baal, for Asherah,[a] and for all the host of heaven;[b] and he burned them outside Jerusalem in the fields of Kidron, and carried their ashes to Bethel. ⁵ Then he removed the idolatrous priests whom the kings of Judah had ordained to burn incense on the high places in the cities of Judah and in the places all around Jerusalem, and those who burned incense to Baal, to the sun, to the moon, to the constellations, and to all the host of heaven. ⁶ And he brought out the wooden image[c] from the house of the LORD, to the Brook Kidron outside Jerusalem, burned it at the Brook Kidron and ground it to ashes, and threw its ashes on the graves of the common people. ⁷ Then he tore down the ritual booths of the perverted persons[d] that were in the house of the LORD, where the women wove hangings for the wooden image. ⁸ And he brought all the priests from the cities of Judah, and defiled the high places where the priests had burned incense, from Geba to Beersheba; also he broke down the high places at the gates which were at the entrance of the Gate of Joshua the governor of the city, which were to the left of the city gate. ⁹ Nevertheless the priests of the high places did not come up to the altar of the LORD in Jerusalem, but they ate unleavened bread among their brethren.

Have you committed to clearing your home and your life of all things that are not of God? Explain Yes or No.

_____
_____
_____
_____
_____
_____
_____
_____
_____
_____
_____

Day 362

Amos 8 (New King James Version)

*⁹ "And it shall come to pass in that day," says the Lord G*OD,
"That I will make the sun go down at noon,
And I will darken the earth in broad daylight;
¹⁰ I will turn your feasts into mourning,
And all your songs into lamentation;
I will bring sackcloth on every waist,
And baldness on every head;
I will make it like mourning for an only son,
And its end like a bitter day.

*¹¹ "Behold, the days are coming," says the Lord G*OD,
"That I will send a famine on the land,
Not a famine of bread,
Nor a thirst for water,
*But of hearing the words of the L*ORD.
¹² They shall wander from sea to sea,
And from north to east;
*They shall run to and fro, seeking the word of the L*ORD,
But shall not find it.

My thoughts about this scripture

_____
_____
_____
_____
_____
_____

What do you believe is meant by "Famine of the word of the Lord"?

_____
_____
_____
_____
_____

(Be sure to ask your Pastor if you are not sure)

Day 363

Romans 14 (New King James Version)

⁵ One person esteems one day above another; another esteems every day alike. Let each be fully convinced in his own mind. ⁶ He who observes the day, observes it to the Lord;[a] and he who does not observe the day, to the Lord he does not observe it. He who eats, eats to the Lord, for he gives God thanks; and he who does not eat, to the Lord he does not eat, and gives God thanks. ⁷ For none of us lives to himself, and no one dies to himself. ⁸ For if we live, we live to the Lord; and if we die, we die to the Lord. Therefore, whether we live or die, we are the Lord's. ⁹ For to this end Christ died and rose[b] and lived again, that He might be Lord of both the dead and the living. ¹⁰ But why do you judge your brother? Or why do you show contempt for your brother? For we shall all stand before the judgment seat of Christ.[c] ¹¹ For it is written:

"As I live, says the LORD,
Every knee shall bow to Me,
And every tongue shall confess to God."[d]

Do you think we judge our brother in hopes that we may make ourselves not look so bad?

_____
_____
_____
_____

If God knows our heart, should we be more concerned about how we feel about people or about what we do for people? (Example, you can care but never help)

_____
_____
_____
_____
_____

My thoughts about this scripture

_____
_____
_____
_____
_____
_____
_____

Day 364

John

[16] For God so loved the world that He gave His only begotten Son, that whoever believes in Him should not perish but have everlasting life.

Deuteronomy

*[5] You shall love the L*ORD *your God with all your heart, with all your soul, and with all your strength.*

*[13] You shall fear the L*ORD *your God and serve Him, and shall take oaths in His name. [14] You shall not go after other gods, the gods of the peoples who are all around you [15] (for the L*ORD *your God is a jealous God among you), lest the anger of the L*ORD *your God be aroused against you and destroy you from the face of the earth.*

*[16] "You shall not tempt the L*ORD *your God as you tempted Him in Massah. [17] You shall diligently keep the commandments of the L*ORD *your God, His testimonies, and His statutes which He has commanded you. [18] And you shall do what is right and good in the sight of the L*ORD*, that it may be well with you, and that you may go in and possess the good land of which the L*ORD *swore to your fathers, [19] to cast out all your enemies from before you, as the L*ORD *has spoken.*

*[6] "For you are a holy people to the L*ORD *your God; the L*ORD *your God has chosen you to be a people for Himself, a special treasure above all the peoples on the face of the earth. [7] The L*ORD *did not set His love on you nor choose you because you were more in number than any other people, for you were the least of all peoples; [8] but because the L*ORD *loves you, and because He would keep the oath which He swore to your fathers, the L*ORD *has brought you out with a mighty hand, and redeemed you from the house of bondage, from the hand of Pharaoh king of Egypt.*

Day 365

Write what you feel you have accomplished in this year of growth.

_____
_____
_____
_____
_____
_____
_____
_____
_____
_____
_____
_____

Express your love for Christ and your new understanding of how He loves you.

_____
_____
_____
_____
_____
_____
_____
_____
_____
_____
_____
_____
_____

May God continue to bless you, for you have established a strong bond and intimate relationship with Christ that we truly hope blossoms into what God has planned for you.

We read that;

"Eye has not seen, nor ear heard,
Nor have entered into the heart of man
The things which God has prepared for those who love Him."[c]

Stay obedient so you don't miss what He has prepared for you,

Thank you and again, God Bless you!

Thank You;

To God,

My Lord and Savior for the many blessing You have placed in my life. I truly believe You are my inspiration and the drive that directs my writing. Without You I am nothing but with You I have accomplished much. I know You have only begun to use me and my desire to write for Your glory.

My Wife Sherri,

I could write for days and not completely express how much I love you. The Bible tells us that God knows us better than we know ourselves and His giving me you proves that.

To our children Tashia, Jonathan, Dominique, Darius, Matthew

For your understanding, confidence and support, you are truly a gift from God and I thank Him for you constantly.

My Mother Mary,

Because of you I am well grounded in Christ. I may not have always followed Him but you assured me He was there waiting to embrace me.

To my church families;
Friendship Missionary Baptist Church (present)
Insoul Baptist Church (former)

Thank you for the support and words of encouragement (and for buying the books) {{smiling}}

If you are not covered by either of these

Thank You....

We may not have met but we share the same Father. Our paths may never cross but we are on the same journey. We may never hear each other's voice but we pray the same prayers. And when this world is over, we will dwell in the same Kingdom. So although we've never met, we know each other well.

God Bless You!

ANSWERS TO PUZZLE PAGE 56 – DAY 55

H¹	A²	L³	S⁴	A⁵		A⁶	G⁷	C⁸	Y⁹		M¹⁰	A¹¹	K¹²	E¹³
A¹⁴	V	I	A	N		F¹⁵	A	R	O		C¹⁶	L	A	D
T¹⁷	E	M	P	T	A¹⁸	T	I	O	N		G¹⁹	I	B	E
E²⁰	R	A	S	E	D		N²¹	A	D	A²²		B²³	U	M
				S²⁴	I	C²⁵		T²⁶	E	Q	U²⁷	I	L	A
S²⁸	P²⁹	A³⁰		E³¹	O	S³²		R³³	U	N				
C³⁴	A	R		S³⁵	U	M	A³⁶	C		I³⁷	T	E³⁸	M³⁹	S⁴⁰
A⁴¹	L	I	K⁴²	E		E⁴³	R	A		L⁴⁴	O	R	A	N
B⁴⁵	E	A	U	X		T⁴⁶	A	M	P⁴⁷	A		A⁴⁸	G	O
			D⁴⁹	I	S⁵⁰		H⁵¹	E	R			S⁵²	I	B
L⁵³	O⁵⁴	C⁵⁵	U	S	T	S⁵⁶		L⁵⁷	I	B⁵⁸				
A⁵⁹	I	R		T⁶⁰	U	T	U⁶¹		M⁶²	A	R⁶³	T⁶⁴	H⁶⁵	A⁶⁶
P⁶⁷	L	E	A⁶⁸		C⁶⁹	O	N	F⁷⁰	E	S	S	I	O	N
S⁷¹	E	E	N		C⁷²	O	D	A		E⁷³	V	E	N	T
E⁷⁴	D	D	Y		O⁷⁵	D	O	R		S⁷⁶	P	R	E	E

THANK YOU TO CHRISTIAN BIBLE REFERENCE SITE

WWW.CHRISTIANBIBLEREFERENCE.ORG OR WWW.TWOPATHS.COM

Daily Nourishing,

Getting closer to Christ one day at a time

Published by: Andy C. Bethea

Date: March 30, 2012

ISBN: 13: 987-1475115178
      10: 1475115172

Written by: Andy Bethea

Made in the USA
Columbia, SC
21 June 2021